HOW TO HOLD YOUR JOB

HOW TO HOLD YOUR JOB

*by Stanley E. Fudell and
John R. Peck*

*The John Day Company
New York*

Contents

		Page
	Preface	7
	Introduction	13
I	*Why Should You Learn about Jobs?*	17
II	*Getting Along with Fellow Workers*	41
III	*Are You Willing to Work and Do Your Best?*	61
IV	*Following Directions and Finishing Your Work*	81
V	*Being on Time*	103
VI	*Are You Reliable? Can We Depend on You?*	123
VII	*Honesty Is Still the Best*	145
VIII	*How to Get a Raise in Salary*	167
IX	*Fifty Ways to Lose Your Job*	187
X	*Cooperation Is the Basis of Success*	195
XI	*Your Attitude Means Success or Failure*	213
XII	*Going for Your First Job Interview*	233

1419645

Preface

ALL TEACHERS of retarded pupils have asked themselves: "What subject matter can I teach these students?" and "What would be the most effective method of presenting the material?" The problem of creating a meaningful curriculum is magnified for the teacher of adolescent retardates. This book is a teacher's answer to such questions as these. It could represent the transition from failure to success.

We faced our first problem of providing a meaningful curriculum in a junior high school class of retardates. Our first effort was a watered-down academic curriculum. The students, a typical group of teenage retardates, reacted to this book-centered curriculum with a sobering lack of enthusiasm. Throughout the year there were many anxious moments of self-doubt and uncertainty on our parts, although the administrators of the school considered it a successful year because a high degree of discipline was maintained and virtually no problems had to be referred to the office. Frankly, we were not pleased with the pupils' disenchantment toward our misguided educational venture. Most of the students made some gains in academic achievement and social maturity, but we honestly could not claim credit for this advancement.

In a subsequent assignment, to open the school system's first high school class for retarded students, we were faced with the same curriculum problem. This class of high school retardates was a fairly typical one. Intelligence quotients ranged from 50 to approximately 75, with a ratio of two boys to one girl. Included in the group were retardates with a familial history of retardation, culturally deprived individuals who performed on individual I.Q. tests at a retarded level, a student or two who showed symptoms of organic brain injury and had major learning problems, and an occasional student who was emotionally disturbed and/or socially maladjusted. All the students had one quality in common: academically they functioned at a retarded level, and most of them also functioned at a

7

depressed social level. In terms of their use of academic tools for
learning purposes, the class performed within the range of serious
subnormality. It was for these students that we had to construct a
curriculum that would be motivating in the classroom and valuable
in later life.

What to teach was the question, and how to teach it so that the
students would be motivated to *want* to learn. We were ashamed
to offer a third-grade reader to a seventeen-year-old adolescent, who
obviously was not interested in two small children and their dog.
Nor could we effectively base a curriculum on watered-down high
school subject matter which was beyond the students' capabilities.

These students were approaching adulthood. In two or more years,
they would be "graduated," and would be expected to compete in
a modern technological society. At this time we began developing
practical units of curriculum based on answers to pertinent questions.
The units were an outcome of approximately five years of questioning, answering, teaching and refinement. In order to determine what
subject matter was most meaningful for retardates, the develop-
ment of the units traversed four steps.

First, we surveyed the available literature. The literature con-
sistently repeated that the success or failure of adult retardates in
our socioeconomic world depends primarily on their ability to
obtain and hold jobs. However, holding a job depends chiefly on
work attitudes and positive traits of personality. A retardate's failure
on the job is usually a result of his inability to adjust his thinking
to the demands of holding a job. The literature delineated some of
the broad aims and objectives, but no specific subject matter was
found that would be appropriate for retardates in their first work
experience.

The second step was to seek specific content that would be valuable to retardates entering the workaday world. After seeking answers in the academic world and receiving little in the way of
practical information, it became obvious that the answers lay with
the employers of retardates. A questionnaire was adapted and was
presented to forty-five employers, and we began the third phase
by attempting to answer the question: What can we teach retardates
to help them hold a job?

Interviews with the forty-five preselected businessmen who employed or had jobs suitable for retarded individuals constituted our third step. The information received was practical, coming as it did from employers who hired or supervised jobs commensurate with the abilities of retardates. The advice obtained from these forty-five employers led to the formulation of the twelve units of instruction that make up this book.

The fourth step was to write lesson plans and student participation material and to refine this course of study as it was used. After several years of refinement, the units were tested under controlled, university-supervised research conditions. The results indicated that these units were indeed instrumental in bettering retardates' work attitudes and values (Fudell in Dissertation Microfilms, 1963). These twelve units are, therefore, a direct outcome of the ever-present question: What do we teach teenage retardates?

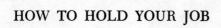

HOW TO HOLD YOUR JOB

Introduction

ONE of the primary objectives of an educational program for teenage retardates is to prepare them for holding productive jobs. The information contained in these twelve units is designed to shape the thinking and behavior of retarded students, so that they will develop the values and attitudes that are basic and necessary to the success of any worker. No attempt is made to teach specific trade information, but rather to impregnate the students with the positive attitudes and thinking that are common to almost any successful job-holder. Each unit is divided into twelve days of classroom work and should span three weeks. This allows one day per week for review material, loss of school time, or "catch-up" time. The titles of the units themselves indicate the objectives of this curriculum material.

Reading Level of the Units

All student reading material in the units is written on a second-grade reading level. For present purposes, any student who has successfully completed a second-grade basal reader is presumed to be reading at second-grade level. All student reading vocabulary in the units appears in either the Dolch Basic Word List, the Ginn, and/or the Scott Foresman basal readers up to and including the second grade. When vocabulary above the second-grade level is used, it is included and presented as new material. This reading level should be within the ability of most retarded teenagers. It is assumed that students using these units will have some skill in adding prefixes and suffixes and in combining known reading vocabulary words. A pupil who is a nonreader should not be excluded from participation, however, for the value of these units is in the information presented and not in their relation to the reading ability of a particular student.

Suggestions to the Teacher

1. Always place the nonreaders in one group and have the material read to them. One of the better reading students can perform

this task for you. Do not exclude them because of lack of ability to read.

2. Be enthusiastic. Most teachers of retardates have experienced at times a boredom with the information itself and the repetition that is needed to teach retardates. Try not to let this boredom affect your enthusiasm. "As you go, so goes the class." The goal of a good teacher of retardates is to inculcate facts—by the use of ingenuity and the employment of many different approaches and techniques.

3. Always explain directions carefully, especially on test days.

4. Try to maintain the units' contents and philosophy continuously in daily class life. Wherever possible, the material should be made a 24-hour living experience. Transfer the principles of the units into other subject matter. Ingrain these ideas, values and habits into the student's total individual behavior while he is in school.

5. You will note that much of this material is presented in question-and-answer form. This technique has not often been used with retarded students. The writers have found it to be an excellent technique for presenting new material, however, and strongly recommend that you try to use genuine showmanship and enthusiasm, or the success of this question-answer technique will be minimized. You may have to probe for a desired answer. At times you will have to skirt inadequate responses until you receive the required answer. When a correct answer is received that is similar to the unit's wording, it should be written on the board. By such reinforcement, students will feel that these answers are theirs. It will mean more to the students if you can say, "But you said this, not I," when reviewing past work or when pursuing new material.

6. If you have working students in your classes, use them to reinforce the material presented. For example, when comparing the difference between being late for school and late for work, reinforce this concept by directly asking a working student the questions, "What happened to you when you were late to school?" and "What would happen to you and your job if you often came to work late?" This student's answer not only will reinforce your teaching but has the added advantage of coming from the student's peer and not from a propagandizing teacher.

7. You will notice that even though the reading material is at a second-grade level, the verbal exchange between students and

teacher approximates an adult level. Keep in mind that most re-tardates' conversational level exceeds their reading level. Do not talk down to your students; wherever feasible, treat them as mature partners in the presentation of these units.

8. Students should be told and encouraged to keep their work-books for use in adult life. Constant review of the material contained in their workbooks will help them to function better as adults in the outside world. Their workbooks can serve as a reference library and answer many of the questions that will arise later in their lives.

UNIT I

Why Should You Learn about Jobs?

Time required: Twelve teaching days

I. Introduction

For the rest of the school year the teacher and the students will be using these units and workbooks on working attitudes and values. If motivation can be maintained continuously, it will lead to a more wholesome learning situation. The aim of this first unit is to provide the students with motivation for the study of the units. If the students' interest lags in later weeks, any one day of this unit can be utilized as a "hypodermic dose" of motivation. An explanation of why they are studying this material on job attitudes will unfold during the teaching of this first unit. Some information concerning occupational education will be imparted to the students, but the primary goal is to instill in the students the concept that this material will be valuable and meaningful to them now and also in the future.

II. Objectives

A. Teacher objectives

1. To motivate the student to desire to study these twelve units.

2. To provide practical material, which the student can use in later life.

3. To provide an awareness of why this material is and will be valuable to the student.

B. Pupil objectives

1. To be motivated to want to study this subject matter.

17

2. To understand why this material is and will be of value when he assumes his role in the workaday world.
3. To be provided with an avenue of discussion within his own peer group on the subject matter. Often the teacher will have to motivate, prompt and lead these discussions.
4. To desire to develop personality traits, values and attitudes which will be beneficial to him in later life.

UNIT I   DAY 1

Why Should You Learn about Jobs?

I. Subject: Story "Ben and Bob: Which One Are You Like?"
II. Purpose
    A. To read a story about Ben and Bob which introduces the material in the twelve units.
    B. To introduce the new reading vocabulary used in Unit I.
III. Materials
    A. Teacher materials
       1. Blackboard and chalk
    B. Student materials
       1. Workbook, "Read This," page 2, and the story "Ben and Bob: Which One Are You Like?" Unit I, Day 1, page 3
IV. Sequence of lesson
    A. Teacher activities
       1. Have students take out workbooks and turn to page 2. Read aloud selection titled "Read This" to students. Students who are able should read along silently with teacher. Introduce the reading with the explanation that this story tells them what they will be studying in this workbook.
       2. Read the story "Ben and Bob: Which One Are You Like?" Have students read along silently while you read story aloud. Introduce story with the following explanation:

"This true story is about two men named Bob and Ben. Both of them were students in a class just like this class.

Ben is earning his own way while Bob still takes money from his father and mother. Which one do you want to be like when you finish school? You will notice that there are many words that are underlined. There are twelve new words we will have to learn. After we finish reading the lesson I will put the twelve words on the board. Tomorrow we will take six of the new words and learn them. We will be using these words all during the year in these units. Later on in this unit we will study the other six words."

B. Student activities
   1. After reading the story, ask students the following questions:

      a. Who that you know is like Bob?
      b. Who that you know is like Ben?
      c. Which person do you think is a better person, and why? (Solicit answers to show that Ben earns his own way, buys his own clothes, saves money, maybe has a watch or car, and is liked and respected by other people.)

   2. Place twelve new words on board. Use the following listing:

We will study these tomorrow:

grade	boss	salary
test	questions	important

We will study these later in the unit:

tools	student	depend
honest	cooperate	attitude

Ben and Bob: Which One Are You Like?

Ben and Bob are brothers, but they are not alike. When they were both in school Ben was a good student, made good grades, did well on his tests, and asked good questions. He knew school was important. The teacher could depend on him, he was honest, had a good attitude, and cooperated with other people. He was the kind of person you want to be.

Bob was very different from Ben. When Bob was a student in high school he didn't care at all about school. He missed school, he came late, he did not listen, and he was almost thrown out of school many times. Bob thought school was for kids. He wanted to go out and find a job and work for a boss and make a salary so he would have money to buy things.

Ben and Bob both finished high school and found jobs. Ben went to work as a dishwasher. He used the same attitudes on his job that he used in school. He had listened and learned the things in school that would help him keep his job. He did the right things in school so he would know what to do when he went to work.

Bob had never learned the right things in school. He lost his job because he broke some tools. He didn't know what was important to hold a job. Bob hasn't been able to keep a job. The sad part is that he wants to work and make money but he has never learned how. He has not learned what he needs to know to hold a job.

Almost everyone wants to get a job and pay his own way, but many people just don't know how. Will you be a Bob or a Ben? This book will help you become like Ben. It will tell you what to do and how to keep a job. You must begin to learn and do these right things now, while you are in school. It will be too late to learn how to hold a job once you leave school.

UNIT I   DAY 2

Why Should You Learn about Jobs?

I. Subject: New reading vocabulary

II. Purpose
To learn new reading vocabulary which is introduced in the story "Bob and Ben: Which One Are You Like?" and which will be used in Unit I and also in subsequent units.

III. Materials
    A. Teacher materials
        1. Blackboard and chalk
    B. Student materials
        1. Workbook, Day 2, page 3
        2. Pen or pencil
        3. Elementary dictionary

IV. Sequence of lesson
    A. Teacher activities
        1. Teacher reads aloud the story "Ben and Bob: Which One Are You Like?" with students and emphasizes new words.
        2. Teacher says, "Yesterday when we read this story we noticed all the new words which are underlined. We

put the twelve words on the board and today we will study six of them. The six words are: grade, boss, salary, test, questions, important. We will be using these six words from now on. They are important words and we must learn them."

3. Drill students on six words.

B. Student activities

1. Teacher says, "In your workbook at the bottom of page 3 and the top of page 4 you will find these six words. Print each word three times."

2. "On a separate sheet of paper I want you to alphabetize the words and find their definitions in your dictionary. After each word write a simple definition so you know what each word means." (Allow ample time for students to look up words. Then write words on the board and ask students for their definitions. Reword their definitions to match the definitions shown below:

Boss: The man we work for. The boss pays our salary.

Grade: Our teacher gives us a grade to show how we are doing in school.

Important: Something that means a lot to us. If it matters to us what happens, it is important.

Questions: When we're not sure about something we ask a question about it, so that we can be sure.

Salary: The money we make on our jobs. Our salary is the money our boss pays us.

Test: A set of questions trying to find out what we know about something. We get a high grade on the test if we know a lot of the questions, and a low grade if we don't know many of the questions.

V. Summary

Teacher says, "I want you to copy these definitions from the board into your workbooks on page 4. At the end of this unit I will ask you to use them in sentences or give a simple definition of each new word. Tomorrow and the next day we are going to compare a day at school and a day on a job, working. Think about it so you can help me and the class decide what is different or the same about a person going to school or going

to work. Study these new words tonight so you know them well.
We will be using them tomorrow."

UNIT I   DAYS 3 AND 4

Why Should You Learn about Jobs?

    I. Subject: The differences between school and work
   II. Purpose
      A. To introduce the pupil to the world of work.
      B. To compare a school day with a work day.
  III. Materials
      A. Teacher materials
         1. Blackboard and chalk
         2. Listing of "How Different Are School and Work?"
      B. Student materials
         1. Student workbook, pages 4, 5, 6 and 7
         2. Pen or pencil
  IV. Sequence of lesson: Unit I, Day 3
      A. Teacher activities
         1. Teacher says, "Each one of us hopes to get a job someday
and earn his own money after he finishes school. Have
you often wondered what it's like to have a job and go
to work every day? Certainly! We all have. However,
what we are doing here can compare to holding a job.
This place that we all know about might be a good place
to start. I mean our school. Every one of us goes to
school." (Solicit answers from students to questions as
shown in workbook Days 3 and 4. When answers are
given, reword them to fit the listing shown below and
the main headings listed in students' workbooks and then
write them on board. If no answers are forthcoming,
prompt and lead discussion. Leave sufficient room below
each school listing to add listing of work comparisons.)
      B. Student activities
         1. After listing is completed, allow ample time for students

to copy work from board into their workbooks on pages 4 and 5. Then say, "We will finish this tomorrow."

V. Sequence of lesson: Unit I, Day 4; students' workbooks, pages 6–7.

    A. Teacher activities

        1. Teacher says, "Yesterday we started to compare school and work. We were able to show only four ways in which school and work were not the same. Today we'll continue this listing because many of you had some good ideas we did not have time to put on the board and let you copy. Before we start, let's read the four things we had put in our workbooks yesterday on pages 4 and 5. This will remind us of what we want to say today." (Follow same procedure as in Day 1, soliciting answers, placing answers on board, and providing ample time for students to copy material from board into their workbooks on pages 6 and 7.)

UNIT I   DAYS 3 AND 4

How Different Are School and Work?

(Workbook, pages 4, 5, 6 and 7)

  I. Being on Time

    School 1. We must come to school on time every day. If we're late too often, we may have to stay in but we won't be thrown out of school.

    Work 1. We must be at work on time every day. If we are late, we will be thrown off our job.

        Different. It's not the same.

  II. Coming Every Day

    School 2. We should be in school every day. If we are not here, we miss our schoolwork and do poorly in our work. Our friends cannot count on us.

    Work 2. If we often miss work, we get fired and lose our jobs and we lose our salary.

        Different. It's not the same.

III.   Doing Our Work
School 3. If we don't do our schoolwork and are lazy, our teacher will grade us down, but we can still come to school.
Work   3. If we don't do our work on a job and are lazy, the boss will fire us and we lose our salary and money.
Different. It's not the same.

IV.   Talking Back
School 4. If we talk back to the teacher, we are sent out of the room and most times when we learn to be nice we can come back.
Work   4. On a job if we talk back to the boss, he fires us. We can't come back. We lose our salary.
Different. It's not the same.

V.   Asking for Help
School 5. If we don't understand our schoolwork, we can ask the teacher to keep helping us.
Work   5. On a job we must listen and understand what to do. We can't keep running back to the boss for more help on the same work. He would soon get tired of us and fire us and we'd lose money and salary.
Different. It's not the same.

VI.   Getting Along
School 6. If we don't like the people in our class, we can stay away from them most of the time.
Work   6. If we don't like the people we work with, we cannot stay away from them; we must work with them. If we can't get along with our fellow workers, we get fired and lose money.
Different. It's not the same.

VII.   Being a Good Worker
School 7. If we work hard and keep working hard, we can get better grades.
Work   7. If we work hard and keep working hard, we can get a raise in salary and that means more money to us and more salary.
Different. It's not the same.

VIII.   Doing Your Best

School 8. If we don't like school and don't do our best, we can still stay in school.

Work   8. If we don't like our job and don't do our best, we get fired and lose our salary and the money that comes with it.

Different. It's not the same.

VI. Summary

Closing statement by teacher for Unit I, Days 3 and 4:

"These differences we have listed on the board in the last two days are only a few of the ways that jobs are different from school. There are many other ways that school is different or the same as working. We shall learn more about these during the school year. Notice that we haven't said anything about why they are different and how we can learn to become people who will do the right things so we can hold our jobs. We hope to learn this later on. If you want to become the kind of person who can hold a job and earn his own salary and the money that comes with it, listen carefully in school. You can learn a lot about being a good worker and keeping your job. Learn these things and practice them here in school. They are the same things you need to hold a job.

"You should have copied this information into your workbook on pages 4 and 5, Unit I, Day 3 and pages 6 and 7, Unit I, Day 4. At the end of this unit, I will ask you questions about the material and give you a test on this work. You will be able to use your workbooks for the test. Learn this work well. It will help you to become a good worker. Later on, after you graduate from school, you can use your workbooks to remind you how to be a good worker and keep your job."

UNIT I   DAY 5

Why Should You Learn about Jobs?

I. Subject: Why Bob can't hold a job
II. Purpose: To illustrate and review in story form the differences between going to school and working.

III. Materials
    A. Teacher materials: none
    B. Student materials
        1. Workbook, Unit I, Day 5, page 7, the story "Bob Is Out of Work Again."
IV. Sequence of lesson
    A. Teacher activities
        1. Teacher says, "Bob is out of work again. The authors of this book asked his boss why he fired him from his job and put his reasons into this story."
    B. Student activities
        1. Students and teacher read story aloud and teacher asks the following questions upon completing the story:
            a. What would you think of someone who came to school late two days out of four days?
            Answer: You could not depend on him.
            b. What do you think about Mr. Smith when he said no to letting Bob make up his late time?
            Answer: Mr. Smith was right. You open and close a business at regular times. A late worker can't stay in and make up the time lost.
            c. What do you think about Bob's attitude?
            Answer: He doesn't seem to care about his job. Maybe he just did not know the right way to hold a job.

Bob Is Out of Work Again

My name is Mr. Smith and Bob worked for me for four days. Why did I let him go? Well, there were several reasons. First of all he came to work late two days of the four he worked for me. On one of the days I needed him to help me do some hard work, and he was a half hour late. When I asked him why he was late he said he got up late and missed his bus. Getting up late and missing a bus is not a good reason for a man to use for being late. He wanted to stay later and make up the time but we close at the same time every day and I wasn't about to stay later so he could make up the time. He just didn't seem to care about his job. He tried, but he did not take care of his tools. I could not depend on him to be on time every day, and he had a poor attitude toward his job. He just did not seem to know what a good worker should know to keep his job.

V. Summary
Teacher says, "Tomorrow we are going to look at our own attitudes toward work. Each of us is going to grade ourselves on

how we work at school. This will help tell us what kind of
worker we are ourselves."

UNIT I   DAY 6

Why Should You Learn about Jobs?

  I. Subject: A student self-rating scale
 II. Purpose: To enable the students to rate themselves on the eight
     characteristics of a good worker in school.
III. Materials
     A. Teacher materials
        1. Blackboard and chalk
     B. Student materials
        1. Rating Scale, workbook, page 8
        2. Pencil
 IV. Sequence of lesson
     A. Teacher activities
        1. Teacher says, "Today we are going to judge ourselves on
           the eight things we studied on days 3 and 4. This is a
           test of ourselves to see what kind of student worker we
           are. Open your workbooks to page 8 and we'll take the
           test together." (Read rating scale and explain criteria at
           the top to students.)
     B. Pupil activities
        1. Allow each student to rate himself.
  V. Summary
     At conclusion of rating test have students add up their scores
     and teacher decides which scores are above or below average.
     Stress the fact that they are going to rate themselves in the
     future. The important thing is to see if there is any improve-
     ment during the year, and if they can better their scores by
     learning this material.

Your Self-Rating Scale

Things I Do:	Always 5	Most of the Time 4	Sometimes 3	Once in a While 2	Never 1
Come on Time	✓				
Come Every Day	✓				
Do My Work	✓				
Try Not to Talk Back		✓	✓		
Ask for Help		✓			
Get Along					
Am a Good Worker	✓				
Do My Best	✓				
MY SCORE:					

UNIT I   DAY 7

Why Should You Learn about Jobs?

I. Subject: Review of Days 1 through 6
II. Purpose: To review information presented in Unit I, Days 1–6.
III. Materials
    A. Teacher materials
       1. Blackboard and chalk
    B. Student materials
       1. Workbook, pages 8 and 9
       2. Pen or pencil
IV. Sequence of lesson
    A. Teacher activities
       1. Teacher says, "For the past several days we have been
          studying some important differences between going to
          school and going to work. We listed these on the board,
          read about Ben and Bob and talked about these dif-
          ferences. Today we want to see if we can list the right
          and wrong way to do these things and what happens to

us in school or on a job if we do these things wrong or right. There were eight ways we talked about. What were these?" (List the eight ways that going to school or work are different. Follow listing shown below.)

B. Pupil activities
   1. Solicit answers from students and change their wording to correspond with wording shown below. Use working students to reinforce student answers.

V. Summary

Teacher says, "If you can remember these eight ways to be a better worker, they will help you the rest of your lives. These eight things can be used on almost anything you do. Whether you are mowing the grass at home or doing some work in school, you will do these things better by trying to follow these eight rules."

(Workbook pages 8 and 9)

Eight ways in which going to school is different from going to work:
   1. Being on Time: Late for school—we stay in; late for work— we get fired.
   2. Coming Every Day: Miss school and we do poorly on our schoolwork; miss work and we lose our jobs.
   3. Doing Our Work: Lazy in school, poor grades; lazy on our jobs, we get fired.
   4. Talking Back: Talk back in school and we may get sent out of class; talk back on a job and we are fired.
   5. Asking for Help: In school we can ask for lots of help; on a job we cannot ask for help all the time.
   6. Getting Along: In school we can stay away from people we don't get along with; on a job we must work with everyone.
   7. Being a Good Worker: In school if we are not good workers we get poor grades; on a job if we are not good workers we lose our jobs.
   8. Doing Our Best: If we do not do our best in school we can still stay in school; if we do not do our best on a job we lose our job.

UNIT I   DAY 8

Why Should You Learn about Jobs?

  I. Subject: New vocabulary
 II. Purpose
     A. To review Day 1 and Day 7.
     B. To introduce new vocabulary.
III. Materials
     A. Teacher materials
        1. Blackboard and chalk
     B. Student materials
        1. Extra paper and pen or pencil
        2. Workbook Unit I, Day 1, page 3; Day 7, pages 8 and 9
        3. Elementary dictionary
 IV. Sequence of lesson
     A. Teacher activities
        1. Teacher says, "Let's reread Unit I, Day 1 and Day 7,
           in your workbook." While reading the story "Ben and
           Bob: Which One Are You Like?" in workbooks, remark
           that there were twelve new words and write them on
           board. (See Day 1 for twelve words.) At end of reading,
           teacher adds, "I'd like to explain the reasons behind be-
           ing a good worker or a poor worker but we don't have
           the time now. Probably some of you are beginning to
           think of the reasons behind these questions. However, I
           can promise you that we will study all these again and I'll
           try to explain all the reasons behind being a good or poor
           worker later on during the year."
     B. Pupil activities
        1. Teacher says, "There are six new words in today's lesson.
           Here they are on the board: tools, student, depend, hon-
           est, cooperate, attitude." (Drill students on vocabulary.)
           "On page 9 of your workbook you will find these six
           words. Write each word three times. On another sheet
           of paper I want you to put these words in alphabetical

order and look them up in your dictionary. Write a simple definition of each word in your own words." (Allow ample time and write definitions of words on board going over them.)

1. Attitude: How you feel about school or work. A good attitude means that you like it and try to do your best.
2. Cooperate: Getting along with your fellow students, teacher or boss. You try to help each other.
3. Depend: You can count on it. They will be there when you need them.
4. Honest: An honest person never takes anything that doesn't belong to him.
5. Student: A person going to school. You are students.
6. Tools: The things we work with. In school our tools are pencils, pens, paper and books. On a job our tools may be a hammer, saw, or a dishwashing machine, or other kinds of tools.
V. Summary
Teacher says, "Copy these words and their meanings into your workbooks on pages 9 and 10. You should be studying your workbooks every night."

UNIT I   DAYS 9 AND 10

Why Should You Learn about Jobs?

 I. Subject: Good and bad workers
 II. Purpose
   A. To list the attributes of good and bad workers and show how this relationship is associated with going to school.
   B. To instill in students the concept that the same attributes are required from both a good student and a good worker.
III. Materials
   A. Teacher materials
     1. Blackboard and chalk

    B. Student materials
       1. Workbook, pages 10–13
       2. Pen or pencil
IV. Sequence of lesson
    A. Teacher activities
       1. Teacher says, "For the next two days we are going to
          make a listing on the board of what you think is a good
          or a bad student and see if this is different or the same
          as being a good or bad worker. Let's start from the time
          we get to school." (Allow space under school listing for
          work listing and for comparison. Use the questions as
          shown below to elicit responses and write responses on
          the board. Use the same questions for school and for
          work with alternate endings. Prompt if necessary and
          reword answers to match those shown below.) "We will
          be using the new words we studied yesterday and last
          week. Let's ask ourselves these questions about coming
          to school and then ask ourselves the same questions about
          going to work and holding a job. Let's see how a good
          or bad student or worker does his job."

Note: Devote the same time and procedure for Days 9 and 10,
student workbook, pages 10–13. Allow sufficient time for a
thorough and complete discussion of each major item listed.
Elicit salient facts from students. Challenge your students to
think and relate their ideas from school to the work world.
Much prompting and motivation will be needed.

UNIT I   DAY 9

A Good Student Will Be a Good Worker

(Workbook pages 10–11)
    1. What is the first thing we must do every day when we come
       to school (or come to work)?
       Good student: Be on time, never late.
       Good worker: Be on time, never late.
               No difference, the same.

    Poor student or worker: Is late, never on time to school (or to work).

2. After we get to school (or to work) what are some of the things we have to do?

    Good student: Be ready for schoolwork—clean, had breakfast, have books, pen and pencil ready, good night's sleep.

    Good worker: Be ready for work—clean, had breakfast, have *tools* ready, good night's sleep.

    No difference, the same.

    Poor student or worker: Dirty, no tools, sleepy, missed breakfast.

3. Now let's get busy in school (or on the job). Am I a willing worker?

    Good student: Yes. Work hard, follow directions, keep working, be awake, keep trying.

    Good worker: Work hard, follow directions, keep working, be awake, keep trying.

    No difference, the same.

    Poor student or worker: Is lazy, doesn't care, is sleepy, gives up easily.

4. Am I at school (or at work) every day?

    Good student: Is at school every day. You can depend on him. If he can't come, he will call and let you know it.

    Good worker: Is at work every day. The boss can depend on him. If he can't come, he'll call and let you know it.

    No difference, the same.

    Poor student or worker: Misses a lot of days. Never calls to let you know. You can't depend on him.

UNIT I   DAY 10

A Good Student Will Be a Good Worker

(Workbook pages 12–13)

5. Am I honest?

Good student: Yes, I never take anything that doesn't belong to me. I work hard for my teacher.

Good worker: Yes, he never takes anything that doesn't belong to him. He works hard for the boss.
No difference, the same.

Poor student or worker: No, he takes things that don't belong to him. You had better watch him and don't leave anything lying around.

6. Do I cooperate with the people around me?

Good student: Yes, I try to help my fellow students and people around me.

Good worker: Yes, he tries to help his fellow workers and people around him.
No difference, the same.

Poor student or worker: No, he doesn't try to help his fellow workers. He makes the people around him dislike him.

7. What kind of attitude do I have toward school (work)?

Good student: My attitude is a good one. I may not like all the things I have to do in school, but I do them and try to be happy about it.

Good worker: My attitude is a good one. I may not like all the different kinds of work my boss tells me to do, but I do them the best I can and try to stay happy at my job. I want people to like me.
No difference, the same.

Poor student or worker: My attitude is a poor one. If I don't like the kind of work my boss tells me to do, I'm not going to do my best. Only if I like the work will I do it well. I don't care if I keep my job or not or if people like me.

8. What kind of people would you like to work with in school (at work)?

Good student: Good people. People who are friendly and helpful.

Good worker: Good people. People who will help me with my work if I need help.

No difference, the same.

Poor student or worker: Bad people. They do not care about you or anyone else. They care only for themselves.

V. Summary

Reread notes on board. At each question pause and ask, "Which kind of student are you? Which kind of worker will you be? You can see that being a good student is almost the same as being a good worker. Put these notes in your workbook on Unit I, Day 9, pages 12 and 13 (Unit I, Day 10, pages 14 and 15). Some of your test questions will come from these notes at the end of this unit. Study these ideas tonight and every night. We will have a test tomorrow on the entire unit. I expect everyone to study for it."

UNIT I DAY 11

Why Should You Learn about Jobs?

I. Subject: Test on Unit I
II. Purpose: To test students' knowledge and grasp of material presented in Unit I.
III. Materials
  A. Teacher materials
    1. Test on Unit I, shown below and on pages 13–16 in students' workbooks.
  B. Student materials
    1. Workbook
    2. Pen or pencil
    3. Notebook, if desired

IV. Sequence of lesson
   A. Teacher activities
      1. Teacher says, "Turn to page 13 in your workbook. The first part of the test is on the new words we learned this week. You will find a list of twelve words and of ten sentences. Pick the right word for the right sentence. Write the correct word in the space left for it. Part 2 on pages 14 and 15 has ten sentences. Each sentence has three answers. Sometimes more than one answer is right. Put a line under the sentence or sentences that are right. Part 3 on pages 15 and 16 is for extra credit. Answer both questions for the extra credit. You won't lose any points if you have a wrong answer on the extra credit. Please use a pencil when taking this test in your workbook." (After test is completed by all students, collect workbooks and grade test. Give back workbooks on Day 12.)

UNIT I   DAY 11

Test on Unit I

(Workbook pages 13–16)

Name————————————————   Date———————————

Part 1

Put the best word with these ten thoughts:

1.	grade	7.	tools
2.	boss	8.	student
3.	important	9.	depend
4.	questions	10.	honest
5.	salary	11.	cooperate
6.	test	12.	attitude

1. When your teacher goes over this paper he will give you a grade on it.

2. When a fellow worker does a good job, and is liked by the people he works with, you can be sure that he has a good attitude.
3. In school your pencils and pens are tools that you use for your work.
4. The man who pays your salary is your boss.
5. When a person comes to work every day and on time you can depend on him.
6. Liking your job is important to you.
7. When you get along with your fellow workers they say that you cooperate with them.
8. If you are not sure about doing something, then you should ask questions and find out what is the right thing to do.
9. The money your boss pays you for working for him is called your salary.
10. People you can depend on not to take anything that is not theirs are honest.

Part 2

Pick the right answer or answers to these questions:
1. If we are often late for school, our teacher can
   A. Fire us.
   B. Stop our salary.
   C. Keep us in after school.
2. If we don't do our work in school we get poor grades, but if we don't do our work on a job our boss will
   A. Give us low grades.
   B. Fire us.
   C. Fire us and we lose our salary.
3. If we work hard in school we can get better grades. If we work hard on our jobs we can get
   A. A raise in salary.
   B. Thrown off our job.
   C. A raise in salary and this means more money.
4. If we don't like the people we have to work with we
   A. Can stay away from them.
   B. Must get along with them.
   C. Must cooperate with them.

5. If we don't like school and are lazy we can still stay in school,
   but if we don't like our jobs and are lazy we
   A. Get a raise in salary.
   B. Might get fired.
   C. Will get fired and lose our salary.
6. A good student or a good worker are both always
   A. On time.
   B. Never late.
   C. Always late and never on time.
7. A good student or worker comes to school or work
   A. Ready and willing to work.
   B. To work hard, and keep a good attitude.
   C. With a good attitude.
8. A poor student or worker comes to school or work
   A. Dirty and sleepy.
   B. Late or doesn't come at all.
   C. Lazy and doesn't work hard.
9. A good student or worker thinks his work or job
   A. Is a question.
   B. Is important to him.
   C. Has a poor attitude.
10. Which one of these is most important to a good worker?
    A. A good attitude.
    B. To ask too many questions.
    C. Not to cooperate.

Part 3

1. Make a list of things that a good student or worker will do in
   school or at work.

1. Be on time	7. Keep trying
2. Be ready to work	8. Be there every day
3. Work hard	9. Be dependable
4. Follow directions	10. Be honest
5. Keep working	11. Cooperate with people
6. Be awake	12 . Have a good attitude

   13. Be a good person

2. Make a list of things that a poor student or worker will do in school or at work.
    1. Be late
    2. Be lazy
    3. Take it easy
    4. Do not follow directions
    5. Be sleepy
    6. Give up when the work is too hard
    7. Do not come every day
    8. Will not be dependable
    9. Take things that do not belong to him
    10. Never help anyone
    11. Have a do-not-care-about-it attitude

UNIT I   DAY 12

Why Should You Learn about Jobs?

I. Subject: Review of test
II. Purpose
   A. To review Unit I by going over test on Unit I.
   B. To allow students to see their mistakes and to correct their wrong answers in their workbooks.
III. Materials
   A. Teacher materials
      1. Test on Unit I
   B. Student materials
      1. Workbook
      2. Pen or pencil
IV. Sequence of lesson
   A. Teacher activities
      1. Return workbooks to students
      2. Review all questions on test. Thoroughly discuss all answers. Explain why one answer is the best of multiple correct answers and why the other correct answers, though correct, are not as good as the first selection.

3. As teacher goes over correct answers, allow ample time for students to correct wrong answers. Thereby, the test serves as a summary of the contents of the unit and can serve as a reference guide in the adult years of the student.

Note: The teacher may question the validity of having the tests on all units in the student's workbook. The test serves as a summary and gathers in all material presented in each unit. If the student refers to test items during the presentation of new content while studying the unit, he is, in effect, learning the material. The teacher should make certain that students are not marking correct answers before the test is administered at the end of each unit. This can be determined by checking the workbooks prior to the test or by occasionally giving the test orally without the workbooks and having the students mark the letter of the correct answer or answers on a separate sheet. Then the test can be given in the workbooks and compared by each student. The teacher can then readily ascertain whether students are marking answers prior to the test.

UNIT II

Getting Along with Fellow Workers

Time required: Twelve days

I. Introduction

A successful employee is usually a person who is able to inter-
act with his fellow workers in an acceptable manner. Any employer is prone to rid his staff of "troublemakers." Retarded
individuals are often retarded to some degree in social interaction. If they can be oriented to an acceptable standard in job
manners and behavior, then this should be an asset to them in
their future social and economic lives. Because they are often
unsure of themselves in social interaction, and especially on a
job, the best role for them to play is one of a quiet, unobtrusive
member of the group. This quiet role is decidedly better for
retardates than a brash, loud, attention-seeking manner.

II. Objectives

A. Teacher objectives

1. To develop desirable attitudes of social deportment.
2. To develop a model of correct social behavior.
3. To develop an awareness of why good, acceptable social
   behavior is necessary for successful personal interaction.

B. Pupil objectives

1. To acquire desirable attitudes of social behavior.
2. To acquire a desirable model of social behavior.
3. To acquire within themselves an awareness of why good
   behavior is necessary for successful living.

41

UNIT II   DAY 1

Getting Along with Fellow Workers

  I. Subject: New vocabulary
 II. Purpose: To teach new vocabulary used in this unit.
III. Materials
  A. Teacher materials
     1. Blackboard and chalk
  B. Student materials
     1. Extra paper and pen or pencil
     2. Elementary dictionary
     3. Workbook, Unit II, Day 1, pages 16–17
 IV. Sequence of lesson
  A. Teacher activities
     1. Teacher says, "The unit we are beginning has to do with
        how we get along with people. Most of us have nice
        manners and get along nicely with other people. In this
        unit we are going to try to learn to be better people on
        a job and how to act on a job so our fellow workers will
        like us and respect us. All of us know people whom we
        like or don't like. However, many of us have never really
        decided why we like or dislike certain people. In this
        unit we are going to study three things." (List on board
        and read to students.)
        1. Why it is important to get along with people.
        2. Why you should want to get along with people.
        3. How to get along with people.
     2. Teacher continues, "Before we can get into the new ideas
        there will be ten new words to learn. Today we will
        study and learn these new words so you can use them
        in this unit." (Teacher reads words and lists on board.)

1.	person	6.	ridicule
2.	reason	7.	stupid
3.	dirty	8.	dumb
4.	neat	9.	date
5.	respect	10.	excuse

        (Drill students on words for reading vocabulary.)

B. Pupil activities
  1. Teacher says, "I want you to put them in alphabetical order on another sheet of paper. When you are finshed we'll put them on the board and check them and then we'll copy them in our workbooks." (Allow ample time. Place list on board and solicit answers to correspond to definitions as shown below.)
     1. Date: When a boy asks a girl to go out with him to a movie, a dance, or a party, he asks her for a date.
     2. Dirty: When you are not clean, you are dirty.
     3. Dumb: When you don't know what you are talking about, or when you talk too much, people say you are "dumb."
     4. Excuse: Something you use when you must leave people, or when you start talking to them. Say "Excuse me, please."
     5. Neat: A clean person who looks nice is a neat person.
     6. Person: You and I are persons.
     7. Reason: Why we do something is the reason we do something.
     8. Respect: If you respect a person, you think a lot of him.
     9. Ridicule: When you make fun of a person, you ridicule him. This is not a nice thing to do.
     10. Stupid: This means the same as "dumb," that you don't know what you are talking about.

V. Summary

When listing is finished, teacher says, "I want you to write these definitions in your workbook on pages 16 and 17. We will need to know these words for this and other units. Be sure you have the correct definitions. Take these words home and study them for tomorrow."

UNIT II   DAY 2

Getting Along with Fellow Workers

  I. Subject: Why should you act nice and have people like and respect you?
 II. Purpose
    A. To teach the concepts of why people develop acceptable behavior.
    B. To enable the student to comprehend that our lives are a continual social interaction with other people and that we cannot live in this world as sole entities.
III. Materials
    A. Teacher materials
        1. Blackboard and chalk
    B. Student materials
        1. Workbook, Unit II, Day 2, pages 17–18.
        2. Pen or pencil
 IV. Sequence of lesson
    A. Teacher activities
        1. Teacher says, "In this unit we are going to study how to get along with other people. Some of you have been thinking that it is important to get along with people because you find that you are a happier person when you do. But *why* are we unhappy when we can't get along with people? What is there *inside* of us that makes us happy or unhappy? Do you think every person in this room has the same feelings about getting along with people? We really don't know. But there may be some reasons that all of us have for trying to get along with people."
    B. Student activities
        1. Teacher says, "Let's ask each person in this room why he thinks it is important for us to get along with other people." (While eliciting answers from students write answers on board and discuss fully. Seek reinforcing

statements from working students. After the listing below
is complete, have students copy material from board into
their workbooks.)

V. Summary

At conclusion of lesson the teacher says, "Tomorrow we will
look at some of the things we like or dislike in people."

UNIT II   DAY 2

Why Should You Act Nice and Have People Like and Respect You?
(Workbook pages 17–18)

I. We like people.
None of us really dislikes other people.
We like some people more than other people.
Every one of us has feelings toward other people.
Most of the time these feelings are good and we want to like
them.

II. Inside of us we want people to like us.
Every one of us wants other people to respect us.
We would be sad persons if we had no one who liked us.
We would think, What's wrong with us?

III. We do not live alone.
All of us have friends.
We could not be happy without friends.
Every day, all day long, we are with people.
We are happier when we like other people and they like us.

IV. It will help us to keep our jobs.
When people like you and respect you, they will help you.
When you work on a job where the people you work with do
not like and respect you, then it will be hard for you to
keep your job.
It is very important for your boss to like and respect you.

UNIT II   DAYS 3 AND 4

Getting Along with Fellow Workers

  I. Subject: What we like or dislike in people
 II. Purpose
   A. To teach the concept of acceptable behavior.
   B. To teach the relationship between acceptable and unacceptable behavior.
   C. To begin to develop an awareness of why the student should accept the correct social role.
III. Materials
   A. Teacher materials
      1. Blackboard and chalk
   B. Student materials
      1. Workbook, Unit II, Day 3, page 18; Day 4, page 19
 IV. Sequence of lesson
   A. Teacher activities
      1. Teacher says, "Every one of us has been around people that we like or do not like. For some reason we like these people or we don't like these people. Have you ever thought of why you like or dislike certain people? Think of some people you like." (Develop these concepts to suit your own method of presentation.)
   B. Student activities
      1. Teacher says, "Let's list on the board the reasons why you do or don't like certain people." (Prompt answers and reword to match listing below. Allow space under "Like" listing for "Dislike" listing.)

UNIT II   DAYS 3 AND 4

Why We Like or Dislike People

(Workbook page 18)

   Like   1. A clean, neat person.
   Dislike   1. A dirty, smelly person.

Like   2. A nice, quiet person. He knows when to talk or be quiet.

Dislike 2. A loud, noisy person. He talks all the time but he doesn't say anything. People don't listen to him.

Like   3. A person who has nice manners. He knows how to talk to people and how to meet people in a pleasant way.

Dislike 3. A person who has no manners. He talks in a bad way and does not know how to meet people. I wouldn't want him to meet my family or girl friend or boy friend.

Like   4. A person who cooperates. He will help you, or be a good person to work with.

Dislike 4. A person who won't cooperate. He won't help you, and he would be a bad person to work with.

UNIT II   DAY 4

(Workbook page 19)

Like   5. A person who respects you. He is nice to you. He thinks of you as a person to be friendly to.

Dislike 5. A person who picks on you. He makes fun of you. He doesn't think very much of you as a person.

Like   6. A person who is always on time. You can depend on him to be there when he is supposed to be there. He's the kind of person you can count on.

Dislike 6. A person who is often late. He makes you wait for him and nobody likes to wait. Sometimes he doesn't even come.

Like   7. A person with a good attitude. He is fun to be with. He is pleasant, and makes good friends.

Dislike 7. A person with a poor attitude. He is sad to be with. He is an unhappy person and makes a poor friend.

Like   8. A friend you really like to be with. He respects you and is nice to you all the time.

Dislike   8. A person who always ridicules you. He makes fun of
              you and says bad things to you.
V. Summary
   Teacher says, "Now that we have listed some of the things we
   like and dislike about people, look at this list we made in the
   last two days. Think of yourself as a person doing these things.
   Would you like or dislike yourself? Remember these eight
   things. If you follow these, you will be liked and be able to
   get along with people."

UNIT II   DAY 5

Getting Along with Fellow Workers

   I. Subject: Story "Ginger and Jane: Which One Do You Like?"
  II. Purpose
      A. To review and reinforce content on good attitudes and be-
         havior in story form.
      B. To compare a good personality versus a poor personality in
         story form.
 III. Materials
      A. Teacher materials: none
      B. Student materials
         1. Workbook, Unit II, Day 5, pages 19–20
  IV. Sequence of lesson
      A. Teacher activities
         1. Teacher says, "Today we are going to read a story about
            two girls who work at the same place. One girl is re-
            spected and the other girl is ridiculed. Let's see if we can
            find out why."
      B. Pupil activities
         1. Read story with students.
         2. Verbally discuss story with students. Compare Ginger
            and Jane to people the students know. Ask the working
            students if there are any people where they work who
            are like Ginger and Jane.

V. Summary

Teacher says, "Tomorrow we are going to read the story again, and see if we can write down the things that make Ginger and Jane the kind of workers they are."

Ginger and Jane: Which One Do You Like?

Ginger and Jane both work at a large cleaning plant. Ginger is well liked and respected by her fellow workers. Let's see how Ginger works and gets along with the people she works with. Ginger always comes to work on time, and she is at work every day. She works with five other girls. She is a hard worker and does her work well. The other five girls can depend on her if they need her help. She is very cooperative. She comes to work looking neat and clean. She is quiet and has very nice manners. She's the kind of girl you would like to be friends with. You would be proud to take her home to meet your family. She has a wonderful attitude about living and is a happy person. Lots of nice boys like to talk to her and take her out on dates. Almost everyone she knows respects her. Wouldn't you?

Jane works at the same cleaning plant, but Jane is not liked. She often comes to work late and sometimes she doesn't even show up. She never telephones her boss when she isn't coming to work. This puts more work on the other girls who work with her. When she does come to work she is dirty looking, not very neat, and she sometimes doesn't smell very nice. People think that she doesn't wash often enough. Her clothes always look as though they need cleaning. You don't need a lot of clothes to be neat and clean.

Jane is a loud-talking person and she never quits talking. She always has something to say but people don't listen to her. Her manners are terrible. When one of the girls she works with needs help, she doesn't help her. She has a poor attitude toward people. She fights with them and says bad things to them. Nice boys don't want to be around her. Everyone thinks the boss will fire her soon. She is no help to herself or the cleaning plant.

UNIT II   DAY 6

Getting Along with Fellow Workers

I. Subject: The reasons for being a good or bad worker
II. Purpose: To compare a good and bad worker in story form.
III. Materials
   A. Teacher materials
      1. Blackboard and chalk
   B. Student materials
      1. Workbook, Unit II, Day 6, pages 20–21
IV. Sequence of lesson
   A. Teacher activities
      1. Teacher says, "Yesterday we read the story about Ginger

and Jane and we talked about the things that made them good or bad workers. Today I want you to turn to page 20 in your workbook and write the reasons why Ginger was a good worker and Jane a poor worker." (Reread the story aloud with students to find the reasons.)

B. Student activities

  1. Teacher says, "I want you to answer these two questions about this story, and then write the answers in your workbook on pages 20 and 21: (1) What made Ginger a good worker, and why was she able to get along with her fellow workers? (2) What made Jane a poor worker, and why wasn't she able to get along with her fellow workers?"

  2. After rereading story aloud, allow students ample time to read story silently and make a listing. Teacher should reread story to nonreaders and aid them in listing. Make listing on board to correspond to teacher's handbook listing and have students correct their listings if they are wrong. Review and discuss the listings.

UNIT II DAY 6

(Workbook pages 20–21)

Why was Ginger a good worker?	Why was Jane a poor worker?
liked	stupid
respected	dumb
on time every day	not respected by fellow workers
never misses work	ridicule her
hard worker	make fun of her
does her work well	comes late often
they can depend on her	misses work
cooperates	never telephones when she misses work
neat and clean	dirty-looking
quiet	not neat
nice manners	smells
wonderful attitude	
happy person	

Why was Ginger a good worker?   Why was Jane a poor worker?

doesn't wash often enough
clothes dirty
loud talking
talks too much
terrible manners
poor attitude
fights with people
says bad things
no help to herself or her job

UNIT II   DAYS 7 AND 8

Getting Along with Fellow Workers

  I. Subject: Avoiding unwholesome social situations
 II. Purpose
   A. To teach the best techniques of interacting with ridiculing people.
   B. How to avoid ridiculing social situations.
   C. How to remove oneself from a ridiculing, loaded social situation.
III. Materials
   A. Teacher materials
     1. Blackboard and chalk
   B. Student materials
     1. Workbook, Unit II, Days 7 and 8, pages 21–22
IV. Sequence of lesson: Day 7
   A. Teacher activities
     1. Teacher says, "During this unit we made a list of things that we liked or disliked about people. Most people are nice. They treat us with respect and we treat them with respect. We can get along with most people all the time.

      "We all know that there are bad people. These people are hard to get along with. They pick on us, they ridicule us, or they make fun of us in front of other people. What they want us to do is talk back to them and to get angry at them. Then they know that their ridicule is not being lost. These people enjoy making other people feel bad. All of us have run into people like these. They will call us stupid, dumb, or just say bad things about us. What can we do so this won't happen, or if it does happen, how can we get away from this kind of person? Think of what you have done when this happens to you."

B. Student activities
1. Teacher says, "Let's list what you have done and see if we can write down a list that we can use or follow. Let's say you are working on a job with many people. One of them likes to ridicule or make fun of you. How would you try to stop this?" (Make listing on board. Solicit answers to correspond to Unit II, Day 7.)

UNIT II   DAY 7

What to do when people make fun of you or do not respect you:
(1) Stay away from this person
    How?
    (a) When you have a break or a rest time, don't go near this person. Talk to someone else. Talk to people who like you and treat you with respect. Or keep to yourself.
    (b) When lunchtime comes, don't eat with this person. Eat with people who like you and who treat you with respect. Or eat alone.
    (c) The thing to do is stay away from this person as much as you can.

IV. Sequence of lesson: Day 8
    A. Teacher activities
    1. Teacher says, "Yesterday we talked about what we could do when we worked with someone who ridiculed us. We talked about how to stay away from this person. What if you work next to this person and you can't keep away from him? What do you do now if he starts to ridicule

you in front of the other workers? You can't walk off your job—if you did you would be fired. What could you do? (Solicit answers from students to correspond to wording shown in Unit II, Day 8.)

UNIT II DAY 8

What if you can't stay away from this person who makes fun of you?
(1) Don't listen to him.
    (a) Let him talk all he wants to. Don't say a word to him. Most of the time your fellow workers will tell him to shut his mouth. He will look like the stupid dumb person.
    (b) If you talk back to him, then you will be the stupid one. When you talk back to him, you are showing everyone that he is right. Don't talk back. Let him do the talking and let him be the stupid one. Remember this is not easy to do. It takes a lot of thinking to be smart and keep your mouth shut.
    (c) What would you do if you are trying to stay away from this person and he walks over to where you are talking to some people and starts to ridicule you? Don't talk back. Say, "Excuse me, please," and walk away. If he follows you to where you are, say, "Excuse me, please," and walk away. He'll stop following you.
V. Summary
Teacher says, "Tomorrow we'll talk about how to keep people from making fun of us."

UNIT II DAY 9

Getting Along with Fellow Workers

I. Subject: How to gain the respect of other people
II. Purpose
    A. To enable the student to establish the concept of what facets of personality make up a wholesome person.

    B. To enable the student to understand the concept that if he is a wholesome person he would not be subject to as much ridicule, and that a positive mental health approach to social interaction is the best preventive for social ridicule.

III. Materials

    A. Teacher materials

       1. Blackboard and chalk

    B. Student materials

       1. Workbook, Unit II, Day 9, page 23

IV. Sequence of lesson

    A. Teacher activities

       1. Teacher says, "For the past two days we talked about what to do when people ridiculed you. The things we studied are very important to know because there will be times when people make fun of other people and you should know what to do. However, there was one idea we did not talk about. You may have thought about this idea. It is how to stop people from making fun of you before they even begin to ridicule you. What we mean is how to get people to respect you so they won't ridicule you."

    B. Student activities

       1. Teacher says, "I want you to think about how to get the respect of your fellow students or workers so they think a lot of you and will not make fun of you. What is the best way to get the respect of people you work with? Let's see what you think the best way is."

       2. Teacher questions students and makes listing to correspond to Workbook listing, Unit II, Day 9, page 23.

 V. Summary

At conclusion of listing have students copy listing from board into workbooks. Review listing and discuss each item fully. Conclude with, "Tomorrow we are going to review Unit I and Unit II. We will have a test in the next few days on Unit I and Unit II."

UNIT II   DAY 9

(Workbook page 23)

The best way to gain the respect of the people you work with:

1. Be clean and neat. Show people that you respect yourself.
2. Be a nice, quiet person. If you have nothing to say, be quiet.
3. Have nice manners. You can learn them by watching people who have nice manners. Do what they do.
4. Be a helpful person. Try to help people.
5. Be friendly to people who respect you. Stay away from people who ridicule you.
6. Be on time, and be at work every day.
7. Have a good attitude. Be happy about life. Be pleasant.
8. Work hard. Show your boss and fellow workers that you are a good worker who earns his salary.

UNIT II   DAY 10

Getting Along with Fellow Workers

  I. Subject: Review Units I and II
 II. Purpose: To review Units I and II
III. Materials
    A. Teacher materials
      1. Test on Unit I
    B. Student materials
      1. Workbook, test on Unit I, Day 11, pages 13–16
IV. Sequence of lesson
    A. Teacher activities
      1. Teacher says, "We are going to review Unit I and Unit II today. Tomorrow we will have a test on Unit II. I want you to study tonight so you will do well on the test."
    B. Student activities
      1. Teacher should review Unit I by verbally going over the

test on Unit I, Day 11, pages 13–16. The test encompasses all important information.

2. Review Unit II by reviewing Unit II, Days 1, 5 and 9.

UNIT II   DAY 11

Getting Along with Fellow Workers

   I. Subject: Test on Unit II
  II. Purpose: To test students' comprehension of material covered in this unit.
 III. Materials
    A. Teacher materials
      1. Test on Unit II
    B. Student materials
      1. Workbook, Unit II, Day 11, pages 24–26
      2. Pencil
 IV. Sequence of lesson
    A. Teacher activities
      1. Teacher says, "We are going to have a test today on Unit II. There will be three parts to the test. Part One is yes and no questions. If you think the thought is right, put a line under the word Yes. If you think it is not right, put a line under the word No. Part Two has sentences with three choices after each sentence. Pick out the right choice and underline it if it goes with the thought. There may be more than one right answer. If there is, underline all the right sentences. Part Three has two questions for extra credit. I will not take off any points from Part Three if you do not answer the questions right. Try them, because any points you make will help your grade. I will collect your workbooks and grade your tests and return them to you in the next few days."
      2. Take nonreaders aside and read questions to these individuals.

UNIT II   DAY 11

Test on Unit II

(Workbook pages 24–26)

Name——————————————— Date———————————

Part 1

Put a line under Yes if you think the thought is right. Put a line
under No if you think the thought is not right.

(Yes) No   1. If we can't get along with our fellow workers we will
get fired.

(Yes) No   2. One of the things we like about people is when they
are nice and they are quiet.

(Yes) No   3. A person with no manners knows how to meet people
and how to talk to them in a pleasant way.

(Yes) No   4. Having a good attitude means that you are a happy
person.

Yes (No)   5. Cooperate means to be bad to people. Not to help
them if they need help.

(Yes) No   6. When you respect a person you like them.

(Yes) No   7. The best way to get people to respect you is to do
your work, be on time, be dependable, and have a
good attitude.

Yes (No)   8. Everyone likes to be ridiculed.

(Yes) No   9. A stupid or dumb person talks a lot but never says
anything.

Yes (No)   10. If I wanted a date with a girl I would ask Jane.

Part 2

Underline all the right answers.
1. When a person ridicules you, you should
   A. Tell your boss.
   B. Tell your fellow workers.
   (C.) Stay away from him.

2. When a person makes fun of you in a group at lunchtime, you should
   √ A. Say, "Excuse me, please," and leave.
   B. Stay there and let him go on.
   C. Keep on eating.

3. When you are working with a bad person and he ridicules you, and you can't excuse yourself, what should you do?
   A. Talk back.
   B. Don't talk back.
   √ C. Keep quiet.

4. If you don't talk back to a person who is ridiculing you, who will be the stupid one?
   A. You.
   √ B. The person doing the ridiculing.
   C. Both of you.

5. When a person is ridiculing you and you keep quiet, it shows that
   √ A. You are smart and using good thinking.
   B. He is a bad person.
   C. He is the dumb one.

6. Ginger was respected by her fellow workers because
   √ A. She was neat and clean.
   B. The five girls she worked with could depend on her.
   C. She had a loud mouth.

7. Which girl would you like to take home to meet your family?
   √ A. Ginger
   B. Jane.
   C. Both.

8. Why don't you need a lot of clothes to be neat and clean?
   A. You can wash them yourself if you want to.
   √ B. It takes very little time to wash clothes so they will be clean.
   C. If you are a dirty person, your clothes will always look dirty.

9. Getting along with your fellow workers means that you must
   A. Fight with them.
   B. Get their respect.
   √ C. Help them when they need your help.

10. Why do you think Ginger will keep her job?
    A. Her good attitude.

√ B. She's a good worker.

C. She is respected by her fellow workers.

Part 3

Answer these two questions. They can help you make a better grade.

1. Why was Ginger good at getting along with her fellow workers?
2. Why was Jane not liked by her fellow workers?

UNIT II   DAY 12

Getting Along with Fellow Workers

I. Subject: Review of unit test

II. Purpose

  A. To reinforce students' grasp of contents of Unit II.

  B. To provide a corrected set of answers to questions on Unit II test.

III. Materials

  A. Teacher materials

    1. Test on Unit II

  B. Student materials

    1. Workbook, Unit II, Day 11, test on pages 24–26

IV. Sequence of lesson

  A. Teacher activities

    1. Teacher says, "We are going over your test on Unit II today. I will discuss each question. If you have an answer that is marked wrong, correct it. When we are finished, you should have all your answers corrected."

    2. Teacher should check workbooks to determine if students have corrected all wrong answers.

V. Summary

Teacher says, "Our next unit is about being a willing worker and doing your best. You can see how each unit goes together with the units we have studied. You should look at Unit III tonight to get some idea of what new information it will teach us."

UNIT III

Are You Willing to Work and Do Your Best?

Time required: Twelve days

I. Introduction

One of the comments most often expressed by employers is that nonskilled employees do not really want to work. Some of their comments ranged from "He's a clock-watcher" to "He's only waiting for payday." Many employers stated that they wished they could get their money's worth in terms of work from their employees. They were not expecting an extraordinary amount of work, but a reasonable amount in relation to salary scales. If the attitude of working hard and trying to do his best at all times can be added to the value system of a worker, it should be a distinct asset to his success in the socioeconomic world. This is especially true of a retarded worker, who often has fewer skills to offer an employer. The objectives of this unit are to instill in students the difference between poor, good and excellent employees.

II. Objectives

A. Teacher objectives

1. To develop in students desirable attitudes toward doing a good day's work.

2. To instill in students the desirable attitude of continuously trying to do their best on a job.

61

      3. To develop in students a model of good working habits in relation to willingness to work.

  B. Pupil objectives

      1. To acquire a desirable attitude toward doing a good day's work.

      2. To learn a model of good working habits in relation to willingness to work, which should help retarded employees be more consistently retained in employment.

UNIT III   DAY 1

Are You Willing to Work and Do Your Best?

  I. Subject: What your boss wants from you

 II. Purpose

  A. To introduce Unit III and its concept.

  B. To introduce new, and review old, reading vocabulary.

III. Materials

  A. Teacher materials

      1. Blackboard and chalk

  B. Student materials

      1. Workbook, Unit III, Day 1, page 27

IV. Sequence of lesson

  A. Teacher activities

      1. Teacher says, "We have studied two units this term. Many of you are wondering where we found this material. Some of you think I made it up. Well, I didn't. We are going to read a story today that tells us where we got this material and why we are studying this material. I think that you will find it is interesting and that it has very little to do with teachers, students or schools." (Read aloud the story "What Your Boss Wants from You.")

      2. After reading the story, discuss briefly the following facts:

         a. These units are not teacher-made.

         b. These units came from industry.

         c. These units will help you hold a job.

3. Then say, "We will reread this story next week and answer questions about it. Read it at home."

4. Then say, "You may have noticed that some of the words were underlined. These are new words that we will study tomorrow."

What Your Boss Wants from You

Some years ago a teacher just like your teacher started teaching a class that was almost like this class. This teacher was trying to get his students ready to get and hold jobs after they <u>finished</u> school. However, he honestly did not know what was important for people to know when they went to work. Someone told this teacher that the best place to find out what to teach was to go to <u>businesses</u> that <u>hired</u> people and ask each boss what he thought was important. The teacher went to 45 <u>businesses.</u> He talked to the people who <u>hired</u> workers and gave them their salaries each <u>week.</u> They told him that the most important thing they looked for in a new worker was his <u>personality</u> and attitude. They wanted these new workers to be able to follow <u>directions.</u> Would these new workers be honest, and give something <u>extra</u> to the work? These bosses wanted people who would listen to directions, and, if they were not sure, ask questions. These bosses were not kidding around. If you were a stupid person and they could not respect you, you were fired. These bosses did not pay off in grades and report cards at the end of a week, they paid money and they wanted people to work for their salaries.

The teacher took this information and put it into the <u>units</u> and <u>sentences</u> you are learning now. No teacher or school made up these units, those bosses did. These are people like the ones you will be working for in the next few years. If you have learned what is in these units, then you will be able to hold a job. If you have <u>not</u> learned them, or if you will not do what these units tell you to do, then you will not be able to hold a job. If you cannot hold a job, then you will stay at home and be a nothing. What you do is up to you. Your teacher can help you, but only you can do the job. No one else can learn what is in these units but you.

UNIT III   DAY 2

Are You Willing to Work and Do Your Best?

I.   Subject: New vocabulary
II. Purpose: To introduce the new vocabulary used in this unit.
III. Materials
   A. Teacher materials
      1. Blackboard and chalk
   B. Student materials
      1. Workbook, Unit III, Day 2, pages 27–28
      2. Elementary dictionary
      3. Pen or pencil, extra paper

IV. Sequence of lesson
  A. Teacher activities
   1. Teacher says, "Yesterday we read a story with nine new words. These are the new words in this unit. They are important words and we will use them from now on." (Teacher reads words to students.)

1. hire	5. finish
2. personality	6. extra
3. week	7. business
4. directions	8. unit

   9. sentence

  B. Pupil activities
   1. Teacher says, "On another piece of paper I want you to put these words in alphabetical order. Find them in your dictionary and write a definition in your own words. When you are finished, we'll go over these words and then you will copy them in your workbooks." (Solicit definitions from students and write definitions to correspond to those shown below. Allow ample time and place list on board with definitions.)
      1. Business: A place that sells or makes things. Stores and cleaning plants are businesses.
      2. Directions: When you are told to do something a certain way, you are getting directions.
      3. Extra: When you do something more than you have to, you are doing extra work.
      4. Finish: When you are through doing something, you are finished.
      5. Hire: Take someone on to work for you. The boss hires you.
      6. Personality: The kind of person you are. A good personality makes people like you.
      7. Sentence: Some words that mean something when they are put together the right way.
      8. Unit: What you are learning in this new work. We put 12 days' work together and call it a unit.

9. Week: Seven days are one week, five days are a school week, five or six days are a work week.
V. Summary
Teacher says, "You should be studying this work and the other work that we have gone over. Are you beginning to see how this material is practical? It will help make you a better person and worker. You should start using these ideas right here in school. If you do them now, they will be easier to follow when you go to work."

UNIT III   DAY 3

Are You Willing to Work and Do Your Best?

   I. Subject: What does a boss hire you for?
  II. Purpose: To teach the students the personality traits a boss looks for when hiring a worker.
III. Materials
    A. Teacher materials
      1. Blackboard and chalk
    B. Student materials
      1. Workbook, Unit III, Day 3, pages 28–29
      2. Pen or pencil
IV. Sequence of lesson
    A. Teacher activities
      1. Teacher says, "Most of you will be looking for jobs when you are finished with school. You will go out and look for jobs. What kind of jobs you look for will depend on what kind of work you want to do. However, all jobs have one thing about them that is the same. This is, what does any boss hire you for? All bosses when they hire workers are looking for the same things no matter what kind of work you will do. I'm asking you to tell us what you think bosses look for. I will make a list of these on the board."
    B. Student activities
      1. Teacher solicits answers to correspond to listing in Unit

III, Day 3, below. At completion of listing, tell students
to copy material from board into their workbooks.

V. Summary

Teacher says, "Tomorrow we will discuss this listing and what
each one of these means."

UNIT III   DAY 3

(Workbook pages 28–29)

Things a boss looks for when he hires workers:
1. Are you willing to work?
2. Are you strong enough to do the work?
3. Your personality and attitude.
4. Do you quit your jobs or are you fired from your jobs often?
5. Can you get along with your fellow workers?
6. Will you try to do your best?

UNIT III   DAY 4

Are You Willing to Work and Do Your Best?

I. Subject: Explanation of things a boss looks for when he hires
workers.

II. Purpose

A. To acquire an awareness of why and what holding a job
entails.

B. To develop the concept of what makes a worker more valuable to his job and employer.

III. Materials

A. Teacher materials

1. Blackboard and chalk

B. Student materials

1. Workbook, Unit III, Day 4, pages 29–30
2. Pen or pencil

IV. Sequence of lesson

A. Teacher activities

1. Teacher says, "Yesterday we studied six things a boss

looks for when hiring workers. We did not have a chance
to explain these. Today we want to look at all six of these
and write in our workbooks what they mean. First let's
put them on the board and see if we all can decide what
these six things really mean."

B. Student activities

    1. Teacher solicits answers from students, rewording them
to fit answers shown in Unit III, Day 4, below. Discuss
each listing fully. Seek reinforcing statements from working students.

V. Summary

After board work is complete, allow ample time for students
to copy information into their workbooks, then say, "Everything
on this list is important but we can't learn about all of them
in one week. However, we are not going to leave any out. We've
talked about Five and we will talk about Three and Four later
on. We can't do much about Two except to look for the kind
of jobs that we can do. That leaves us One and Six to talk about
this week. Write these in your workbook and study them tonight. Tomorrow we'll talk about One, Are You Willing to
Work? and Six, Trying your Best, and how these will help you
keep your job."

UNIT III   DAY 4

(Workbook pages 29–30)

    1. Are you willing to work?

       We'll talk about this all week. Let's leave it for now.

    2. Are you strong enough to do the work?

       You can do very little about this except try to make yourselves
stronger. You can look for jobs that you are strong enough to
do. You wouldn't look for a heavy job if you are not strong
and big. You wouldn't look for a job loading or unloading
trucks if you weren't big and strong.

    3. How about your personality and attitude?

       We will be learning about these things all through the units.
Remember, in the first unit we talked about learning more

about these things. If you listen and work hard, you should
learn how to have a better personality and attitude.

4. Do you quit your jobs or were you fired from your jobs often?
   We will be learning more about these in later units.

5. Can you get along with your fellow workers?
   We learned about this in Unit II. You should go back and
   reread this unit. It is very important.

6. Will you try to do your best?
   We'll talk about this all week. Let's leave it for now.

UNIT III   DAYS 5 AND 6

Are You Willing to Work and Do Your Best?

  I. Subject: The differences between a good and bad worker
 II. Purpose
    A. To teach desirable work characteristics.
    B. To compare a good worker with a poor worker.
III. Materials
    A. Teacher materials
       1. Blackboard and chalk
    B. Student materials
       1. Workbook, Unit III, Days 5 and 6, pages 30–32
IV. Sequence of lesson
    A. Teacher activities
       1. Teacher says, "Yesterday we made a listing on the board
       of what a boss looks for when he hires workers and what
       these meant. Today we will discuss willingness to work
       and trying your best. What do we mean when we say
       'willing to work'? It's more than just working and trying
       hard. There are a lot of things that go with willingness
       to work and trying your best. You tell me what you think
       these mean and I'll list them on the board. First tell me
       how a good worker would be willing to work and try his
       best, and how a poor worker would not be willing to
       work or try his best." (Solicit answers and reword to
       fit list below. This list was compiled from interviews

with employers of unskilled labor. Initiate Day 6 as a
continuation of Day 5.)

2. Teacher says, "You can see that willingness to work
   means and takes a lot of things. All of these are important if you are going to be a good worker. Compare
   them to what a poor worker would do on his job."
   (Emphasize the comparison between the two. Stress
   differences strongly and ask in relation to each question,
   "What kind of worker will you be?")

3. Allow students ample time to copy material into their
   workbooks on both days.

UNIT III   DAY 5

The Differences Between a Good and a Bad Worker

(Workbook page 30)

Good worker   1. Willingness to work—he tries hard and does his
              part of the work.

Poor worker   1. Lazy—he doesn't want to work. He only wants
              his salary. He is a clock-watcher.

Good worker   2. He listens and follows directions. If he is not sure
              what to do, he asks good questions and finds out.

Poor worker   2. He doesn't listen or follow directions. If he is not
              sure what to do, he goes ahead and does it wrong.
              If he asks questions, they are stupid questions that
              he should have known about.

Good worker   3. He gets along with his boss and fellow workers.
              He cooperates.

Poor worker   3. He doesn't get along with his boss and fellow
              workers. He doesn't add anything to the job.

Good worker   4. He finishes the job he starts. He knows what to
              do and he does it.

Poor worker   4. He leaves the job partly finished. Often he doesn't
              know what to do. He doesn't listen to directions.

UNIT III DAY 6

The Differences Between a Good and a Bad Worker
(continued from Day 5)

(Workbook page 31)

Good worker 5. He does not mind when his boss tells him that he is doing something wrong, and shows him the right way to do it. He wants to learn new things about his job and do them right.

Poor worker 5. He doesn't like to be told what to do. He becomes angry when he is told to do something. He has a poor attitude about his job.

Good worker 6. He's interested in the business that he works for. He knows that if he is going to keep his job the business must do well first.

Poor worker 6. He's not interested in the business. He doesn't care if the business is doing well or not. He's only interested in himself.

Good worker 7. He likes his job and the people he works with. He has a good attitude and is happy at work. He adds to the job.

Poor worker 7. He doesn't care at all about his job. He adds nothing to the job and doesn't care about the people he works with.

Good worker 8. He is on time every day, ready to work. You can depend on him.

Poor worker 8. He is late often or doesn't even show up for work. You can't depend on him.

UNIT III DAY 7

Are You Willing to Work and Do Your Best?

I. Subject: Extras your boss likes
II. Purpose
    A. To teach desirable attitudes toward doing extras on the job.
    B. Why these "extras" make a worker more valuable.

III. Materials
    A. Teacher materials
        1. Blackboard and chalk
    B. Student materials
        1. Workbook, Unit III, Day 7, pages 32–33
        2. Pen or pencil
IV. Sequence of lesson
    A. Teacher activities
        1. Teacher says, "So far we have learned what makes a willing worker who tries his best all the time. These are things that any willing or good worker does. However, are there extra things that can make you a better worker? Why would a boss think more of one good worker than another good worker? What does he do that makes him a still better worker? What do you think would make him a still better worker?" (Discuss and list these on board. Prompt if necessary and reword to match listing below. Allow ample time for students to copy information.)
  V. Summary
    Teacher concludes by saying, "These are what we call 'extras'— things a boss likes his workers to do. They make the worker a lot more important to the business. Many workers don't seem to do these things. When they do, it helps them keep their jobs. If you were a boss, wouldn't you like your workers to have these extras?"

UNIT III   DAY 7

Extras Your Boss Likes

(Workbook page 32)

1. A worker is willing to stay on after quitting time to finish a job that the boss needs finished. It means staying over and not getting paid for it. A boss likes this.
2. He keeps busy. When he finishes a job, he doesn't sit around waiting to be told what to do. If there is nothing to do, he cleans up the tools and work place or puts things away.

3. If there is some extra work to do, like unloading a truck, he does his share and more without being asked to help. He sees that there is work to do and he does it.
4. He's honest in his work and never takes anything home that belongs to the boss or anyone else. You can depend on him to be honest. He does a good day's work and he is honest.

UNIT III   DAY 8

Are You Willing to Work and Do Your Best?

I. Subject: Reread the story "What Your Boss Wants from You"
II. Purpose
   A. To reinforce and review source of units.
   B. To review employers' requirements of new employees.
III. Materials
   A. Teacher materials
      1. Blackboard and chalk
   B. Student materials
      1. Workbook, story "What Your Boss Wants from You," Unit III, Day 1, page 27
      2. Pen or pencil
IV. Sequence of lesson
   A. Teacher activities
      1. Teacher says, "On the first day of this unit we read a story called 'What Your Boss Wants from You.' Today we are going to reread this story and then answer some questions about this story. Let's read the story together." After the story has been read, teacher says, "Turn to page 33 in your workbooks. There are four questions. Let us try to answer them. I'll write your ideas on the board and when we all agree on what is right, you can copy them into your workbooks."
   B. Student activities
      1. Students copy listing off board into workbooks.

UNIT II   DAY 8

Questions on the Story "What Your Boss Wants from You"

(Workbook page 33)

1. Where did the things come from that we are learning from these units?
   Bosses who hire people in their businesses.
2. How did the authors get the ideas for these units?
   The bosses said that these ideas were important and would help us keep our jobs.
3. What were some of the things bosses wanted in their new workers?
   1. Have good personality and attitudes.
   2. Follow directions.
   3. Be honest.
   4. Give that extra.
   5. Respect each other.
   6. Listen and ask good questions.
4. What were some of the things that bosses did not want in new workers, so that they fired them if they found them?
   1. Dumb.
   2. Dirty.
   3. Did not listen.
   4. Could not follow directions.
   5. Not honest.
   6. Poor personality and poor attitudes.

V. Summary
   A. Teacher solicits answers to questions and rewords answers to correspond to answers shown above. Discuss all answers fully.
   B. Teacher says, "I think that you'll agree that these units are not the usual school-type material. You'll notice that everything they teach you is practical and the type of thing that you'll need to hold a job. Study this material every evening."

UNIT III　DAY 9

Are You Willing to Work and Do Your Best?

   I. Subject: Personal Rating Scale
  II. Purpose
     A. To allow students to relate good work attributes to their work and attitudes in school.
     B. To allow students to rate themselves on information taught in Unit III.
 III. Materials
     A. Teacher materials: none
     B. Student materials
        1. Workbook, Unit III, Day 9, page 34
        2. Pen or pencil
 IV. Sequence of lesson
     A. Teacher activities
        1. Teacher says, "For the past few weeks we have been studying the differences between a good and bad worker and the extras that a boss looks for in a good worker. Have you wondered how you would rate as a worker if this class were a business and your schoolwork was considered a job? Today each one of us is going to grade himself to see if he is a good or poor worker in this school."
        2. Teacher continues, "Open your workbooks to page 34 and I'll read each line and tell you how to grade yourself. You grade yourself by looking at the top of the page to find the box that tells how you do these things. You'll notice that the left side of the page tells you how to act and the top asks how often you do these things. Then you put in the grade shown in the top box where you think it belongs. I want you to be honest when you grade yourself. Later on this year we'll do this again and see if you have improved or have become a poorer worker."

Rate Yourself. Are You Doing Better?

Things I Do:	Always 5	Most of the time 4	Sometimes 3	Once in a while 2	Never 1
1. Try hard; am not lazy; am a good worker	✓				
2. Listen and follow directions; ask good questions		✓			
3. Get along; cooperate; help out when asked	✓				
4. Finish the job; start a job and finish it	✓				
5. Am willing to be told what to do; don't talk back	✓				
6. Am interested in my work; try to do well	✓	✓			
7. Like my job and the people around me		✓			
8. Come on time everyday; am never late	✓				
9. Am willing to stay extra and finish the job					
10. Keep busy and keep on working	✓				
11. Do extra work without being asked	✓				
12. Am honest; do a full day's work and never take anything home	✓				
MY SCORE:					

V. Summary

  A. After students have graded themselves in their workbooks, tell them to add up scores. From class scores derive an average and relate students' scores to above average, average, or below average. Explain rating scores carefully.

  B. After scores are explained, complete Day 9 with, "Could you hold a job with the scores you made today? You'll notice that the scores you used to rate yourselves can be made into report-card grades: 5 = A; 4 = B; 3 = C; 2 = D; and 1 = F. Would you have received good or poor grades? You ought to think about any grade below a B, and why it is below a B and how you can improve these poor grades. Later on this year we'll rate ourselves again. Will you go up or down? It's really up to you, and only you."

UNIT III   DAY 10

Are You Willing to Work and Do Your Best?

  I. Subject: Review of Units I, II, III
 II. Purpose: To review information learned in Units I, II, and III.
III. Materials

  A. Teacher materials: none

  B. Student materials

    1. Workbook, Unit I test, Day 11, page 13; Unit II test, Day 11, page 24; Unit III, Days 5, 6 and 7, pages 30–32

IV. Sequence of lesson

  A. Teacher activities

    1. Teacher says, "We are going to have our Unit III test tomorrow. Today we will review Units I, II, and III. Take out your workbooks."

  B. Student activities

    1. Review Units I and II tests. Read all questions and discuss fully.

    2. Review Unit III, Days 5, 6 and 7. Discuss material in students' workbooks. Discuss statements and notes students have entered in their workbooks for these days.

V. Summary

When review is completed, say, "Study Unit III carefully to-night. We'll be taking our test tomorrow."

UNIT III   DAY 11

Are You Willing to Work and Do Your Best?

I. Subject: Unit test
II. Purpose
    A. To test students' grasp of material covered in Unit III.
    B. To review and test all vocabulary introduced in first three units.
III. Materials
    A. Teacher materials: none
    B. Student materials
        1. Workbook, Unit III, pages 35–36
        2. Pen or pencil
IV. Sequence of lesson
    A. Teacher activities
        1. Teacher says, "We are having our unit test today. On the first two parts you will have to answer two long questions. On Part 3 you will have to alphabetize 31 words and write as many definitions as you can. The definitions are extra credit. If you get any wrong on Part 3, I won't take any points off. If you get them right, it will add to your grade. You may use your notebooks, if you wish. When you are finished, bring up your paper and read me the alphabetized list of words."

UNIT III   DAY 11

Are You Willing to Work and Do Your Best?

Test on Unit III

(Workbook pages 35–36)

Name——————————————————— Date——————————

Part 1

Make a list of what you think makes for a good worker.

Part 2

Make a list of what you think are the "extras" that make for a better worker.

Part 3

Alphabetize all these words:

1. depend	9. finish	17. attitude	25. hire
2. boss	10. personality	18. cooperate	26. sentence
3. honest	11. week	19. grade	27. unit
4. important	12. directions	20. question	28. extra
5. salary	13. ridicule	21. student	29. stupid
6. dirty	14. reason	22. respect	30. neat
7. dumb	15. tools	23. business	31. person
8. test	16. date	24. excuse	

1. —————   9. —————   17. —————   25. —————

2. —————   10. —————   18. —————   26. —————

3. —————   11. —————   19. —————   27. —————

4. —————   12. —————   20. —————   28. —————

5. —————— 13. —————— 21. —————— 29. ——————

6. —————— 14. —————— 22. —————— 30. ——————

7. —————— 15. —————— 23. —————— 31. ——————

8. —————— 16. —————— 24. ——————

Extra credit. You can't lose. Write as many definitions of these words as you can. You may use your workbooks.

UNIT III   DAY 12

Are You Willing to Work and Do Your Best?

I. Subject: Review of Unit III test
II. Purpose
   A. To review and reinforce students' learning and grasp of Unit III.
   B. To allow students to see their errors on test and allow them to correct wrong answers.
III. Materials
   A. Teacher materials
      1. Blackboard and chalk
   B. Student materials
      1. Workbook, Unit III, Day 11, pages 35–36
IV. Sequence of lesson
   A. Teacher activities
      1. Teacher says, "I have graded your tests and we are going to go over the answers. If you have a wrong answer, correct it. When we are finished, all your answers should be correct. When you study this workbook after you have left school, you know that your answers will be right."
   B. Student activities
      1. Read each question and write the correct answers on the

board. Discuss each question fully. (Allow ample time
for students to copy correct answers into their workbooks.)

V. Summary

Teacher says, "The next unit will be 'Following Directions and
Finishing Your Work.'"

UNIT IV

Following Directions and Finishing Your Work

Time Required: Twelve days

I. Introduction

Many employers have expressed dissatisfaction concerning the performance of workers in their jobs. An often-expressed complaint is, "They don't listen to directions and don't know what to do. So they come back and ask for directions on the very same information that was just explained." As teachers of the educable mentally retarded, we are often faced with this situation in our classrooms. It can be a frustrating situation in class, and a situation that leads to the loss of jobs. If the habits of listening to directions, following through to completion a piece of assigned work, and continuing on to the next piece of work can be inculcated into the working habits of retarded individuals, then they will have developed a strong asset relating to their success.

II. Objectives

A. Teacher objectives

1. To develop in each student desirable attitudes toward following directions.

2. To help students develop desirable attitudes toward listening carefully and asking intelligent questions if the directions are not clear.

81

3. To help them develop desirable attitudes toward completely finishing a piece of work.
4. To develop in students desirable attitudes toward continuing on to further work after present work is completed.
B. Pupil objectives
1. To acquire desirable attitudes toward carefully following directions.
2. To acquire desirable attitudes toward listening to directions and asking intelligent questions if the directions are not clear.
3. To acquire desirable attitudes toward completely finishing a piece of work.
4. To acquire desirable attitudes toward continuing on to further work after present work is completed.

UNIT IV   DAYS 1 AND 2

Following Directions and Finishing Your Work

  I. Subject: Following directions
 II. Purpose
    A. To teach the concept of following directions.
    B. To teach the concept of listening carefully to directions.
    C. To teach the concept of asking intelligent questions when the worker is unsure of directions.
    D. To show the close relationship between these concepts in school and in socioeconomic life.
III. Materials
    A. Teacher materials
       1. Blackboard and chalk
    B. Student materials
       1. Workbook, Unit IV, Days 1 and 2, pages 37–39
       2. Pen or pencil
 IV. Sequence of lesson
    A. Teacher activities
       1. Teacher says, "Today and tomorrow we shall be studying

the ideas of following directions, listening carefully and, especially, asking good questions about the directions if they aren't clear to us and we're not sure what we are supposed to do. There are other things that we'll study in this unit in the next two weeks." (Develop these concepts to suit your own method of presentation.)

2. Teacher continues, "You will notice that I haven't said anything about following directions in any special place, such as on a job or in school. Actually these ideas are the same whether you are on a job or here in school. There have been many times here in school when you did not understand directions or did the wrong things because you didn't listen carefully to what you were told. What happened then? You came to me and I gave you the directions again, or if you weren't listening carefully, you asked silly questions about what I had just told you. I don't like to repeat these directions to you, but I do. If you were on a job and this happened often, how long do you think it would be before you were fired?"

B. Student activities

1. Teacher says, "Today and tomorrow we're going to see how following directions in school is like following directions on a job. We're going to make a listing on the board and see what you need to do to follow directions in both school or on a job." (List both areas at the same time. Place each question on the board and solicit answers from students. Reword answers to coincide with answers below.)

UNIT IV   DAY 1

Following Directions

(Workbook page 37)

I. What does "following directions" mean?

Answer: To learn to do something a certain way. Often we

can't see the reasons for doing it this way, but there is always a good reason. These directions often tell us everything to do from the beginning to the end of a job. Sometimes they are written on paper and at other times they are told to us.

Good student 1. A good student or worker will follow direc-
or worker   tions carefully. He knows that following directions carefully is important. If it weren't important, why would people spend so much time giving careful directions?

Poor student 1. A poor student or worker does not follow
or worker   directions carefully. He does as he wants, and often he does the wrong things.

II. How do you follow directions carefully?

Answer: A. You must listen carefully. When you are told what to do, listen. You must hear what is being said.

B. Look right at the person talking to you. Look him in the eye. Don't stare off into space.

C. Think hard about what is being said. If you are not thinking, then the words don't mean anything to you. Be smart and think, so that you can remember what you are told.

D. Make sure the directions are clear to you, that you understand what to do. If you are not sure, then ask good questions so that you will understand everything.

Good student 2. A good student or worker listens, he thinks
or worker   hard, he remembers, and he asks good questions if he doesn't understand everything about the directions. When he is sure, he goes ahead and does his work right.

Poor student 2. A poor student or worker does not listen or
or worker   remember or understand his directions. He asks foolish questions about what was just said to him. The boss wonders where he was when the directions were given.

V. Summary

Have students copy material from blackboard into their notebooks. Then say, "Tomorrow we'll continue. Study these tonight."

UNIT IV   DAY 2

(Workbook page 38)

    I. Why is it important to follow directions?

       Answer: There are several reasons.

           A. Not to lose your own time. If you do something the wrong way and have to do it over, you waste a lot of your own time. Time is money.

           B. Not to waste material. If you start working on a sheet of paper and it's wrong, you may throw it away. But on a job you cannot waste and throw away a lot of material that costs money. Your boss won't like this at all.

           C. Not to waste other people's time. If you do something wrong and must stop to do it over, you waste your boss's or your teacher's time. If he must give you new directions or tell you again how to do it, he is wasting his time. You waste your time and the boss's or teacher's time. This is time and money lost to the business or school.

Teacher says, "For the past two days we have each given our reasons on how to listen and follow directions. Some of these reasons and ways may be too long for you to remember. Let's see if we can put down the best ways to follow directions in a short list, so that we can remember them." (Question students and elicit the following six answers.)

1. Listen carefully.
2. Think hard.
3. Remember.
4. Understand everything.
5. Ask good questions if you're not sure.
6. Finish the work.

V. Summary
Teacher says, "You can easily see that these habits of following
directions are the same for school and for a job. If you can
learn to follow these habits in school, you can also learn to do
them on the job when you go to work."

UNIT IV   DAY 3

Following Directions and Finishing Your Work

  I. Subject: New vocabulary
 II. Purpose
    A. To review Day 1 material.
    B. To introduce and teach new vocabulary used in Unit IV.
III. Materials
    A. Teacher materials
        1. Blackboard and chalk
    B. Student materials
        1. Extra paper and pencil
        2. Workbook, Unit IV, Day 3, pages 39–40
        3. Dictionary
IV. Sequence of lesson
    A. Teacher activities
        1. Teacher says, "There are eight new words in this week's
           unit. We must learn these if we are to understand all the
           new material we are going to learn about. Here are the
           new words:

1.	raise	5.	waste
2.	certain	6.	material
3.	understand	7.	habits
4.	wrong	8.	cafeteria

           Find these words in your dictionary and write their
           meanings in your own words. Alphabetize these words."
           Allow ample time and place words on the board with
           these meanings:

(Workbook page 39)

1. Cafeteria: A place where people eat and then pay for their food.
2. Certain: Something that is sure—no maybe about it.
3. Habits: When we do things very often, they become easy to do. They become habits. We shall try to learn good habits.
4. Material: By "material" we mean things that are used in our everyday lives. This can be material for clothes. It also means what we learn. There is learning material in these units.
5. Raise: To lift up, to become more. A raise in salary means that we get more money.
6. Understand: To know about something. When we understand something, we know what to do or how it works. We understand all about it.
7. Waste: To let things become useless. If we throw away something that is still good, or if we don't use it correctly and it breaks, then we are wasting it.
8. Wrong: When we are not right we are wrong. The wrong thing is not the right thing.

V. Summary

Teacher says, "Copy these words and meanings into your workbook. Study them tonight. Tomorrow we shall use them in sentences with some of the other words we have learned."

UNIT IV   DAY 4

Following Directions and Finishing Your Work

I. Subject: Review of old and new vocabulary
II. Purpose
   A. To review old vocabulary from Units I, II, III.
   B. To review new vocabulary.
III. Materials
   A. Teacher materials
      1. Handbook
   B. Student materials
      1. Workbook and pencil

IV. Sequence of lesson
   A. Teacher activities
      1. Teacher says, "Turn to page 40 in your workbook. At the bottom you will find a listing of every word we have studied in Units I, II and III, and yesterday's new words. They are all mixed up and I want you to alphabetize them in the spaces on page 41. If you wish to earn some extra credit, after you have alphabetized them, mark after each word the number of the unit where you first learned this word. You can use your workbooks to find which unit the words came from."
   B. Student activities
      1. Students alphabetize words in workbook, page 41. Allow sufficient time for students to complete alphabetization. When students are finished, teacher should read the correct listing and elicit definitions of each word, discussing its use in the unit where it first appeared. As teacher reads corrected list, allow time for students to correct their listing.
V. Summary
   Teacher says, "When I read the correct alphabetized list, some of you had some mistakes. Take your workbook home and practice reading the list to someone in your family. Learn how to read all these words and what they mean. We will be using them in other units."

UNIT IV   DAY 4

(Workbook page 40)

Alphabetize these words first. Then, if you have time, put the number of the unit where you first learned these words:

test	tools	salary	habits
unit	understand	dumb	wrong
boss	question	waste	person
finish	directions	stupid	attitude
student	important	business	week
excuse	reason	respect	extra

raise	personality	honest	dirty
grade	neat	material	ridicule
certain	hire	date	job
cafeteria			

Corrected list: (Teacher)

attitude 1	excuse 2	neat 2	student 1
boss 1	extra 3	person 2	stupid 2
business 3	finish 3	personality 3	test 1
cafeteria 4	grade 1	question 1	tools 1
certain 4	habits 4	raise 4	understand 4
date 2	hire 3	reason 2	unit 3
directions 3	honest 1	respect 2	waste 4
dirty 2	important 1	ridicule 2	week 3
dumb 2	material 4	salary 1	wrong 4

UNIT IV   DAYS 5 AND 6

Following Directions and Finishing Your Work

I. Subject: Keep working, keep busy
II. Purpose
   A. To teach the concept of completing a job.
   B. To teach the concept of continuing to work after a job is finished.
   C. To teach the attitude of keeping busy.
III. Materials
   A. Teacher materials
     1. Blackboard and chalk
   B. Student materials
     1. Workbook and pencil
IV. Sequence of lesson
   A. Teacher activities
     1. Teacher says, "A few days ago we talked about how to follow directions and why it is important to follow directions. Today and tomorrow let's see if we can go to the next step. What do you do when you finish some work?

You have followed directions carefully and finished this job. What do you do next? Can you tell me?" (Write questions and answers down as shown below. Prompt if necessary. Develop these concepts to suit your own method of presentation.)
  B. Student activities
    1. Allow students enough time to copy material from the board into their workbooks.
  V. Summary
    Teacher says, "Tomorrow we shall review this. Study this material tonight."

UNIT IV   DAY 5

Keep Working, Keep Busy

(Workbook page 41)
  1. When you have finished your work, then what do you do? Answer. Find some more work. Keep busy.
    A. If your work is the kind that is the same all day long, keep on working. Don't rest between jobs. Start the next job. If it's the same work over and over again, just keep working. You don't need any new directions. Keep on working.
    B. If your job is one that has different kinds of work, start on the next kind. As long as you have directions to keep working on different jobs, go to the next job. If you are a dishwasher and the busy time is over, and you know that you are to help in the kitchen washing pots, you don't need anyone to tell you what to do, you go and do it. Go into the kitchen and start the next job. Don't rest. Go to the next job.
    C. If you have to wait for new directions for the next job, go and find your boss and tell him you are finished and ask, "What shall I do next?" When he tells you, follow directions carefully. Be sure your job is finished right before you go ask for more work.
    D. If your job is finished and you go to ask your boss for more work and he is busy, what do you do? Don't sit around and

wait. Keep busy. There is always some cleaning to do. Help someone else. Be cooperative. Find some work. Do that extra work. The boss likes this in his workers. Keep busy all day on the job or in school.

UNIT IV   DAY 6

IV. Sequence of lesson
  A. Teacher activities
    1. Teacher says, "Yesterday we talked about working and keeping busy. Let's read this over again. There was a lot of new material covered that was very important." (Reread the material covered yesterday. Emphasize important points and seek reinforcement from working students. At conclusion of reading say, "Can we take all of these good things and make some easy-to-remember rules for us to follow?")
  B. Student activities
    1. Solicit answers from students to coincide with listing shown below and place on board. Allow students ample time to copy into workbooks, page 42.
V. Summary
These five rules are short and simple to read. Encourage some students to make a large poster with these rules on it. Finish day with statement, "If you look at the successful people around you, you'll find that they follow these five rules in their work. Study them and learn to follow them so you can be a good worker."

UNIT IV   DAY 6

(Workbook page 42)

Rules for Working	How to Do It
1. Keep working.	Don't stop.
2. Don't rest.	Keep working.
3. Find more work.	Keep busy.
4. Don't sit around.	Don't be lazy.
5. Do that extra work.	Be cooperative.

UNIT IV   DAY 7

Following Directions and Finishing Your Work

   I. Subject: Story "Ben and Bob"
  II. Purpose
    A. To review the new material in this unit in story form.
    B. To review contents of Days 1 and 6.
 III. Materials
    A. Teacher materials
       1. Blackboard and chalk
    B. Student materials
       1. Notebook and pencil
       2. Workbook, Unit IV, Day 7, page 42
  IV. Sequence of lesson
    A. Teacher activities
       1. Teacher says, "I have a story about Ben and Bob. You
remember, Ben is a good worker and Bob is always
losing his job. Look at why one keeps his job and the
other loses his jobs. What type of worker are you here
in school? What type of worker will you be when you
finish school and go to work? Open your workbooks to
page 42 and let's read the story together."
   V. Summary
Teacher says, "This is a true story. This happens every day.
That is why I want you to learn to follow directions and be good
workers here in school. If you get in the habit of doing good
work in school, you will carry these good habits with you when
you finish school and go to work. For homework tonight I want
you to read this story again and see if you know why Ben kept
his job and why Bob lost his job. Tomorrow we'll look at the
story again and see if we can decide why Ben and Bob were
different on their jobs and which kind of a worker you want to
be."

Ben and Bob

Bob just <u>lost another job.</u> Ben just had <u>a raise in salary.</u> Ben's boss wanted to give him a better job, but Ben can't read or write too well. Ben's boss gave him a small raise anyway. This shows that you can be a respected worker and get raises in salary even if you can't read or write very well. Ben is a good worker, with a <u>good attitude,</u> and that's why <u>his boss respects him.</u> Ben works as a dishwasher in a cafeteria and has three helpers. During the busy hours Ben works at the dishwashing machine, while his helpers clean the front of the cafeteria. When he is finished with the dishes, he goes into the kitchen and washes the pots. <u>He doesn't have to be told to do this.</u> He just <u>goes to the next job he has to do</u>. If he finishes washing his pots before his helpers are finished in the front of the cafeteria, he goes and helps them. If his helpers finish their work before Ben they come and help him. They were <u>given directions</u> to follow when they started working in the cafeteria. They <u>listened and remembered</u> and they all do their job well. They all keep busy and that's why they have had raises in salary. They are good cooperative workers.

Now how about Bob? On Bob's last job he worked at a plant where they made tires. All he had to do was put the tires on a long table so they could be marked. The other workers depended on him to keep enough tires on the table so they could mark them. If he <u>slowed down,</u> then they didn't have enough tires to keep them busy. A lot of workers depended on him to keep busy. <u>Bob didn't last long</u> on this job. He would <u>stop to smoke or sit down</u> and the other workers ran out of tires to mark. If there was a slow time, he would sit down to rest and <u>not try to get ahead</u> in his work. When Bob was in school his teacher tried to make Bob a good worker, but he was <u>lazy</u> and <u>never developed good work habits.</u> When he went to work, his boss fired him and found another worker who would work. No boss is going to pay you a salary to sit around and do nothing.

UNIT IV   DAY 8

Following Directions and Finishing Your Work

I. Subject: Why was Ben a good worker and Bob a poor worker?
II. Purpose
    A. To review story about Bob and Ben, Day 7.
    B. To summarize good and bad work habits of Bob and Ben.
III. Materials
    A. Teacher materials
        1. Blackboard and chalk
    B. Student materials
        1. Workbook, Unit IV, Day 8, page 43
        2. Pen or pencil

IV. Sequence of lesson
   A. Teacher activities
      1. Introduce lesson by saying, "Yesterday we read the story about Ben and Bob. In the story were true reasons why these young men were successes or failures. Today we are going to read the story again. This time, though, as we read the story I want us to pick out the reasons why Ben and Bob were good or bad workers. Every time we find a reason let's put it on the board. At the end of the story, I want you to copy these reasons into your workbooks." Solicit reasons to correspond with the listing below.
   B. Student activities
      Students read story carefully with teacher's guidance and select reasons to put on the blackboard for Ben's and Bob's success or failure. At conclusion of listing, students copy list into their workbooks, page 43.

UNIT IV   DAY 8

(Workbook page 43)

Why was Bob a poor worker?
1. lost his job
2. not dependable
3. slow worker
4. stopped to smoke
5. sat down and rested
6. didn't last long
7. other workers had to do his job
8. went to rest room at wrong times
9. did not try to get ahead
10. lazy
11. bad working habits

Why was Ben a good worker?
1. raise in salary
2. boss respected him
3. good attitude
4. didn't have to be told to work
5. went to the next job and helped
6. listened and remembered directions
7. good cooperative worker
8. hard worker
9. kept working

V. Summary

Teacher says, "Which one of these men would you want to work with? Tomorrow we're going to rate ourselves and see what kind of workers we are in school."

UNIT IV   DAY 9

Following Directions and Finishing Your Work

I. Subject: Rate yourself on your work—are you a good or bad worker?

II. Purpose

A. To enable the students to put to practical use the contents of Unit IV.

B. To reinforce contents of Unit IV.

III. Materials

A. Teacher materials: none

B. Student materials

1. Workbook and pencil

IV. Sequence of lesson

A. Teacher activities

1. Teacher says, "For the past two weeks we have been talking about following directions and work habits. Many of you have been sitting here writing these ideas into your workbooks. Today we are going to use these ideas in a useful way. Each one of you has a rating form in your workbook, page 44. I will explain how to mark it and rate yourself. After you are finished marking your own form, we'll add them up and see how you rate compared to other people in this class."

2. Explain rating scale carefully and read each line to students as they grade themselves. Emphasize that they may put only one tally mark on each line.

B. Student activities

1. Students rate themselves on rating form.

Rate Yourself on Your Work

Things I Do:	Always 5	Most of the time 4	Sometimes 3	Once in a while 2	Never 1
Listen carefully to directions		✓			
Remember directions		✓			
Ask good questions if I'm not sure		✓			
Do not waste my time	✓				
Do not waste material	✓				
Do not waste other people's time	✓				
Have good working habits	✓				
When finished I find more work			✓		
Keep busy	✓				
Do not rest except at break		✓			
Finish a job all the way	✓				
Work hard	✓				
Cooperate and help other people	✓				
Am dependable—come every day	✓				
Am respected by other people	✓				
On time every day	✓				
MY SCORE: 80					

V. Summary
When students have completed their rating forms, explain how to arrive at a score. Add numbers in corresponding lines and divide by 16. Teacher adds students' scores and arrives at an average for class. Explain to students what their scores mean in relation to class average.

UNIT IV   DAY 10

Following Directions and Finishing Your Work

I. Subject: Review of Unit IV
II. Purpose
  A. To review and reinforce contents of Unit IV.
  B. Prepare students for unit test.
III. Materials
  A. Teacher materials: none
  B. Student materials
    1. Workbook, Unit IV, Days 1, 2, 5 and 6
IV. Sequence of lesson
  A. Teacher should review information in Unit IV, Days 1, 2, 5 and 6. Go over each day carefully in a manner similar to original day's teaching schedule. Emphasize important points via the question-answer technique. Allow students to use workbooks during review. This review can also serve to allow the students to rectify incorrect answers. The four days included in the review material contain the important concepts of Unit IV.
  B. Teacher says, "Today we are going to review Unit IV for the test tomorrow. Listen carefully and check the answers in your workbooks. If you have a wrong answer, correct it."
V. Summary
Teacher says, "Everyone should have the correct answers in his workbook on the lessons we reviewed today. I want you to study all of Unit IV tonight because we are going to take a test on this unit tomorrow. If you can't read this unit by yourself, ask someone in your family to help you."

UNIT IV   DAY 11

Following Directions and Finishing Your Work

  I. Subject: Unit test
 II. Purpose
    A. To test the pupils' grasp of the new information in Unit IV.
    B. To test the pupils' grasp of important concepts of past units.
III. Materials
    A. Teacher materials: none
    B. Student materials
      1. Workbook, page 45
      2. Pencil
 IV. Sequence of lesson
    A. Teacher activities
      1. Teacher says, "Today's test is divided into three parts.
        Part 1 has some sentences with three answers. Some of
        the sentences have more than one right answer. Under-
        line all the answers that are right. Part 2 has some ques-
        tions. Answer all questions in Part 2. Part 3 is a review
        test on Units I, II and III. You may use all your notes
        when you take this test."
      2. Teacher should read test to nonreaders.
  V. Summary
    Teacher should collect workbooks and grade test.

Test on Unit IV

(Workbook pages 45–47)

Name———————————————— Date——————————

Part 1

Underline all the right answers to these questions and sentences.
  1. Following directions means:
    A. To do as you please.

B. To do something the way your boss or teacher tells you to
do it.

C. Not to do anything.

2. The first thing to do when following directions is:

A. Don't listen.

B. Look as though you are listening.

C. Listen very carefully and think hard.

3. One reason that it is very important to follow directions is:

A. That you don't waste your time.

B. That you don't waste your boss's time.

C. That you don't waste material.

4. Why is following directions in school the same as following
directions on the job?

A. By following directions, you learn good habits.

B. A good worker never follows directions.

C. Following directions anywhere shows you have a good attitude and are a good worker.

5. To get a raise in salary means that:

A. Your boss is paying you more money.

B. You are about to be fired.

C. You are a good worker.

6. When you understand something you:

A. Ask stupid questions about it.

B. Do not listen to directions.

C. Know about it and know what to do.

7. When you are finished with a job you should:

A. Rest and sit down.

B. Keep working.

C. If there is no work, find some and keep busy.

8. Before you start any new work, you must be sure that:

A. This job is all finished.

B. This job is not done half way.

C. You did the job right.

9. If you do not follow directions you can:

A. Lose your job.

B. Get a raise.

C. Waste money and time.

10. A good worker listens carefully to directions:

    A. So he will not know what to do.
    B. So he can be a good worker.
    C. So he will know what to do.

Part 2

Answer these two questions.
1. List the five things to do or not to do after you are finished with your work.
    1. Keep working.
    2. Don't rest.
    3. Find more work.
    4. Don't sit around.
    5. Do that extra work.
2. List the six important things to do in following directions:
    1. Listen carefully.
    2. Think hard.
    3. Remember.
    4. Understand everything.
    5. Ask good questions if you're not sure.
    6. Finish the work.

Part 3—Review

If the sentence is right, put a circle around the word Yes. If the sentence is wrong, put a circle around the word No.

Yes No   1. If we don't do our work in school we get poor grades, but if we don't do our work on a job our boss will fire us.
Yes No   2. A willing worker tries hard and has a good attitude.
Yes No   3. A poor worker is not interested in his job or the business he works for.
Yes No   4. The extras you do on your job make you more important to the business you work for.
Yes No   5. An honest worker works hard all day long and never takes anything that does not belong to him.
Yes No   6. When a person ridicules you, try to stay around him.
Yes No   7. A worker who is respected always has a good attitude and cares for his job.

Yes No 8. One of the things we like about people is that they are nice and quiet.

Yes No 9. Cooperate means to be bad to people.

Yes No 10. I would like to work with Jane because she is a good worker and dependable.

UNIT IV   DAY 12

Following Directions and Finishing Your Work

I. Subject: Review of test
II. Purpose
   A. To review contents of Unit IV.
   B. To review contents of Units I, II and III.
   C. To allow students to correct wrong answers.
III. Materials
   A. Teacher materials: none
   B. Student materials
      1. Workbook and pencil
IV. Sequence of lesson
   A. Teacher activities
      1. Return graded tests in workbooks to students and go over each question carefully. Much good teaching can take place during a lesson of this nature. Allow ample time for students to correct tests.
   B. Student activities
      1. Students read questions and answers with teacher elaborating on each question. Students should correct wrong answers.
V. Summary
   Teacher says, "You should all have the right answers to all the questions. Study them during the next units. They will also be valuable to you after you graduate and are holding jobs. The next unit will cover 'Being on Time.'"

UNIT V

Being on Time

Time Required: Twelve days

I. Introduction

One of the uncompromising demands that employers make of their employees is punctuality. A tardy employee does not engender strong feelings of confidence and reliability in the employer. In addition, there is loss of respect and confidence on the part of fellow workers. This loss of respect and confidence usually causes other problems, which may lead to the dismissal of the tardy worker. Educable mentally retarded youth need all their positive assets working for them in order to be successful individuals in their later lives. If the attitude of trying to be on time can be inculcated in their value systems, this would be one more asset to aid their success. The importance of punctuality cannot be overstressed in relation to being an effective person.

II. Objectives

A. Teacher objectives

1. To develop in each student a desirable attitude of punctuality.

2. To provide an opportunity for group discussion related to punctuality.

3. To develop an awareness of why people should be on time.

4. To demonstrate that punctuality in school leads to punctuality on the job.

B. Pupil objectives
   1. To acquire desirable attitudes toward being on time.
   2. To discuss with the peer group the pros and cons of punctuality.
   3. To develop in themselves an awareness of why it is important to be on time.
   4. To develop in themselves the desire and habit of being punctual.

UNIT V   DAYS 1 AND 2

Being on Time

  I. Subject: Being on time for school and job
 II. Purpose
    A. To teach desirable attitudes toward being on time.
    B. To show the relationship of being punctual in school life to being punctual in a working situation.
    C. To develop the concept, through pupil participation, of the basic relationship of punctuality between school life and work life.
III. Materials
    A. Teacher materials
       1. Blackboard and chalk
    B. Student materials
       1. Workbook, Unit V, Days 1 and 2, pages 48–49
       2. Pen or pencil
 IV. Sequence of lesson
    A. Teacher activities
       1. Teacher says, "Each one of us has some reasons as to why we should always be on time. Every day we have to be at certain places at certain times, or do certain things at certain times. For example, we have to get up every school day at a certain time to get ready for school, eat breakfast, and be here early enough so we won't be tardy. In your everyday lives, think of the things that

you must do or the places where you must be at certain times. Today and tomorrow we are going to make a list of these on the board, so we can see how many times each day all of us have to be on time. [Leave space below school listing for workday comparisons.]

"Now let's say that every one of us has a job and we go to work every day. Would having a job change our having to be on time so very much? Do you think that going to school or going to work every day are so different? Let's take each thing we wrote on the board and see how much we would have to change from going to school to going to work." (List work comparisons under school and note differences or similarity, soliciting answers from pupils.)

Note: Each day after this comparison of school and work has been made, continue, "We can all see how little difference there is in being on time when we are going to school and when we are going to work. You can see that being on time is very important to each one of us. In the next few days we'll talk about why we must be on time."

B. Student activities

1. Teacher says, "I want you to copy these notes into your workbook. We will call this day's notes Unit V, Day 1 or Day 2, so if we want to look at them again, we'll know where to look. I'm going to ask you questions and give you tests later on in the unit and if you need to, you will be able to look at your workbooks for answers. The important thing to remember for today is: Being on time for work is almost the same as being on time for school." (Write this on board after notes.)

UNIT V DAY 1

Being on Time for School and Job

(Workbook page 48)

School 1. Getting up in the morning on time.
Work   No different. It's the same.

School   2. Eating breakfast.
Work   No different. It's the same.

School   3. Getting to our bus or ride on time.
Work   Getting to our jobs on time. No different. It's the same.

School   4. Being in class before the tardy bell.
Work   Being on our jobs on time. No different. It's the same.

School   5. Changing classes on time.
Work   We don't change jobs—different. It's not the same.

School   6. Going to lunch on time and coming back on time.
Work   No different. It's the same.

School   7. Leaving school on time so we can catch our bus or ride.
Work   Sometimes staying on to finish some work—little difference. Almost the same.

UNIT V   DAY 2

(Workbook page 49)

School   8. Getting to our jobs or to our home on time after school.
Work   We stay on our jobs until it's quitting time. Different. It's not the same.

School   9. Doing our after-school work at home or our after-school jobs in a certain time.
Work   We work all day at one job. Different. It's not the same.

School 10. Finishing our jobs in time to be on time for supper, so our family won't have to wait for us.
Work   We stay at our jobs until quitting time, or until we finish some work. No different. It's the same.

School 11. Doing our homework and other work after supper so we'll have time to get ready for bed.
Work   No homework. Different. It's not the same.

School 12. At home, there is a certain time to use the telephone or watch TV or just play.
Work   No different. It's the same.

School 13. Bathing, or rolling up our hair time.
Work   No different. It's the same.

School 14. Getting to bed on time so we can get a good night's sleep.
Work   No different. It's the same.
V. Summary
Teacher says, "You see that every one of us has a certain time that we have to do something. None of us can go through the day without having to be on time. Each one of us must be on time or at certain places each day and every day."

UNIT V   DAYS 3 AND 4

Being on Time

 I. Subject: Why we should always be on time (in two parts)
 II. Purpose
   A. To personalize work for Days 1 and 2.
   B. To develop the concept of why we should always be on time.
III. Materials
   A. Teacher materials
     1. Blackboard and chalk
   B. Student materials
     1. Workbook, pages 50–52
     2. Pencil
IV. Sequence of lesson
   A. Teacher activities
     1. Have students open workbooks to Day 1 notes. Again using format of Day 1, go over notes. Stress the similarities of being on time for a school situation and the working situation. Ask the following questions of class; if answers are not forthcoming, prompt class.

UNIT V   DAY 3

Why We Should Always Be on Time—Part 1

(Workbook page 50)

1. Why is it important to get up on time when going to school or going to work?
    Answer: So we won't be late for school or work.
2. What happens if we miss our bus, or ride, to school or work, or start out too late?
    Answer: We will be late for school or work.
3. Is this good or bad? Why?
    Answer: Bad. Many people depend on us to be on time.
4. What happens if we are late for lunch?
    Answer: We might miss eating our lunch or have to hurry.
5. Why should we be on time for supper?
    Answer: Our family is waiting for us. If we are late, they have
    to wait for us.
6. If we are working on a job, when would it be good to work a little longer and be late for supper?
    Answer: If our boss wants us to stay to finish up something
    we started. If there is no need to stay on our job past
    quitting time we should go home.
7. Why should we start getting ready for bed at the right time?
    Answer: So we can get cleaned up and in bed at the right time
    and get a good night's sleep.
      2. Teacher says, "We have seen how being on time for
          school or work are almost the same. Which do you think
          is more important, being on time for school, or being on
          time for work? Actually, each is just as important as the
          other. In school we try to learn the habit of being on
          time so when we go out to work on jobs we will have this
          habit of being on time and just keep doing it in our jobs.
          You might say that being on time for work is more
          important because on a job if we are late too often the
          boss or employer will fire us. Then we have no jobs and

no money coming in. In school if we are late too often we may have to stay in after school but we don't get fired or lose our jobs. Now let's talk about why we have to be on time when we do go out and find jobs and go to work."

UNIT V DAY 4

Why We Should Always Be on Time—Part 2

(Workbook page 51)

1. If you were a boss or employer and one of your workers often came in late, what would you think of him?

   Answer: 1. He doesn't care for his job.
   2. I sure can't depend on him.
   3. He's holding up some of the other workers.
   4. If I let him come in late and don't fire him, maybe some of the other workers will start being late to work.
   5. Maybe I'd better fire him and get someone who will be on time and someone that I can depend on.

2. When you are working on a job and you work with someone who is late to work in the morning, or late to work after lunch, or late to work after a break, what do you think of this person?

   Answer: 1. He sure doesn't care about his job. If he did, then he would be on time.
   2. I sure wouldn't like to work with him because if he's late, then we get behind in our work and the boss might think it's because of me and I might get fired.
   3. I sure don't think much of that person. Every time he is late it's almost like taking something away from our boss, and that's not the right thing to do.
   4. He says that his mother doesn't wake him on time, but that's no reason to be late. He's grown up and should wake himself.

      5. I just don't think much of him. I don't care if
he gets fired.

      6. I don't want him for a friend. Every time we'd
make a date to meet he would be late, and I
certainly wouldn't take that very long.

  B. Student activities

    1. Allow ample time for students to copy material into
workbooks.

V. Summary

Teacher says, "Tomorrow we will study a few new words and
review some words that you are having trouble with. Look
through your word lists in each unit and find the words you
are not sure of. I will try to help you learn them."

UNIT V   DAY 5

Being on Time

  I. Subject: New vocabulary

 II. Purpose

  A. To define and learn new words that do not occur in second-
grade vocabulary.

  B. To review important vocabulary in Units I, II, III and IV
which students are unsure of.

III. Materials

  A. Teacher materials

    1. Blackboard and chalk

  B. Student materials

    1. Workbook and pencil

    2. Dictionary

IV. Sequence of lesson

  A. Teacher activities

    1. Teacher says, "There are three new words in this unit
that you will have to learn. The new words are employer,
bus and mature. I want you to look up these words in
your dictionaries. Write a simple definition of each word

in your workbooks, page 53, so you will know what they mean."

2. Teacher says, "After we have finished with these three new words, I want you to be ready with the old words that are troubling you. We'll review them." (Teacher should pass among students and help them with old, troublesome words.)

B. Student activities

1. Students look up words and write definitions. Teacher then places words on the board, eliciting the following definitions from the students:

    1. Bus: A big car—we pay money to ride in it.
    2. Employer: Our boss, the man we work for, is our employer.
    3. Mature: A mature person is a grown person, who acts right and knows what to do.

2. Teacher says, "We will be using these words in other work. Learn them now. Copy these into your workbooks."

UNIT V   DAY 6

Being on Time

I. Subject: Being on time for work
II. Purpose: To review in story form the concepts of being on time.
III. Materials
   A. Teacher materials: none
   B. Student materials
      1. Workbook, Unit V, Day 6, pages 53–54
IV. Sequence of lesson
   A. Teacher activities
      1. Teacher says, "Today we are going to read another story about Ben and Bob. As you must have guessed, Bob still has his problems. As we read this story, try to understand why Ben and Bob are so different. Tomorrow we'll go over the story and try to list what Ben and Bob did that made them good or bad workers."

B. Student activities
   1. Students read story aloud. Teacher emphasizes important
     points.
V. Summary
   Teacher says, "Tonight I want you to read the story. If you
   can't read it by yourself, ask someone in your family to help
   you."

Being on Time for Work

Ben and Bob both work. Ben keeps his job, but Bob always loses his in a short time. Read on and see if you see why Ben keeps his job and why Bob is always losing his job. Ben has to be at work at eight o'clock in the morning. When his clock wakes him at six in the morning he gets up and gets ready for work. He eats breakfast and catches the seven o'clock bus. He has a job as a dishwasher in a cafeteria, and he has three helpers who work with him on the same dishwasher. Ben gets to work early enough so he has enough time to change his clothes and be at his dishwasher machine by eight o'clock. Ben is well liked at the cafeteria. He is always on time. His boss can depend on him to be there every day at the right time. His three helpers know they can depend and count on Ben to be on time and to do his work. Ben started out as a helper, but he was given the head job when his employer saw what a good worker he was.

Now let's see what kind of worker Bob is. Bob works in a bakery and his job is washing up all the pans. He is only a helper, and he works under a head pan washer. He has to be at work at eight o'clock in the morning. When the clock wakes him at six in the morning he doesn't get right out of bed like Ben. His mother has to keep on waking him, but he always gets up late, often misses breakfast, doesn't clean up very well, and often misses his bus. Two or three days a week he is late to work. When he is late, the head pan washer has to do his work. Bob is not liked by his boss or by the people who work with him. They can't depend on him. By being late so often he isn't a very good worker.

You can see by the way they act that Ben is a mature person and Bob is an immature person. A mature person does what he has to at the right time. An immature person is still like a child. He won't do what he has to by himself and depends on others to do things for him. Employers don't keep immature people working for them.

UNIT V   DAY 7

Being on Time

  I. Subject: Are you "a Ben" or "a Bob" kind of worker?
 II. Purpose: To review and reinforce the reasons for Ben's and
    Bob's success or failure at work as depicted in the preceding
    day's story.

III. Materials
   A. Teacher materials
      1. Blackboard and chalk
   B. Student materials
      1. Workbook, Unit V, Days 6 and 7, pages 53–55
      2. Pencil
IV. Sequence of lesson
   A. Teacher activities
      1. Teacher says, "Yesterday we read a story about Ben and Bob. I will read it again today and see if we can decide why Ben was a good worker and Bob a bad worker." Teacher reads story and then asks questions, eliciting answers to coincide with Workbook, Unit V, Day 7. Place answers on board to emphasize important ideas.
   B. Student activities
      1. Students answer questions and write answers in Workbook, Unit V, Day 7, page 54.
V. Summary
   Teacher says, "You can easily see now why Ben was getting raises in salary and why Bob was getting fired from his jobs. You'll notice that the things that make Ben a good worker are habits we can and should build here in school. Get in the habit of being on time. Tomorrow we are going to see how being on time affects each one of you personally."

UNIT V   DAY 7

(Workbook pages 54–55)

   I. What kind of worker will you be, like Ben or like Bob?
      Answer: Ben. He's dependable and well liked by people who work with him.
  II. Why was Ben a good worker?
      Answer: 1. He came to work on time.
              2. He came early enough so he could change his clothes and be on the job on time.
              3. His employer could depend on him.
              4. His three helpers could depend on him to be on time and do his work.
              5. He was liked by the people he worked with.

III. Why was Bob a poor worker?

Answer: 1. He wouldn't get up in the morning so he could get ready for work.
2. He was late too often.
3. The people he worked with had to do his work when he was late.
4. He didn't look clean when he came to work because he didn't get up early enough to get cleaned up for work.
5. He didn't care for his job very much.

UNIT V   DAY 8

Being on Time

I. Subject: How being on time affects you personally
II. Purpose: To reinforce concepts of Unit V by placing them in a personal context for each student.
III. Materials
  A. Teacher materials
    1. Blackboard and chalk
  B. Student materials
    1. Extra paper and pencil
    2. Workbook, Unit V, Day 8, pages 55–57
IV. Sequence of lesson
  A. Teacher activities
    1. Teacher says, "We have been studying being on time all week. Today we are going to see why and how being on time affects each one of you now and in later life."
    2. Write each question outlined below on board and read questions for nonreaders. Write answers below questions. If answers are not readily forthcoming, then prompt and record answers as shown below.
V. Summary
Teacher says, "You can see that each one of you must be on time here at school or later in life when you go to work. The habit of being on time must be learned now, while you are in

school, so you will know what it means to be on time when you go to work. Tomorrow we will review Units I, II, III and IV. I want you to read these four units tonight."

UNIT V   DAY 8

(Workbook pages 55–57)

I. Why is it important to be on time when you are meeting a friend?

Answer: So we won't be late and keep our friends waiting for us.

II. Why is it important to be on time to school (or job)?

Answer: So we will be at school (or job) at the right time and not be late, and start our work on time. We want our teacher (boss) to be able to depend on us.

III. If we are late to school (or job) what will our teacher (employer) think about us?

Answer: 1. Your teacher (boss) will think that you don't care for your job.
2. Your teacher (boss) won't be able to depend on you.
3. You will hold up the people who work with you.
4. The other workers might start coming in late.
5. You will get fired and lose your job.

IV. If we are late to school (or job) what will the people we work with think about us?

Answer: 1. He doesn't think very much about his school (job) or he would be on time.
2. If he's late, then we get behind in our work and the teacher (boss) might think it's because of me.
3. When he's late he takes time away from our teacher (boss) and that's not right.
4. He's grown up now and it's up to him to be on time. He's not a baby now and he can't say that his mother didn't wake him.
5. I don't want to work with him. I don't think much of him.

V. What is the difference between being late for school and being late for work?

Answer: Being late for school means staying after school, being late for work means getting fired and losing money we need.

UNIT V   DAY 9

Being on Time

 I. Subject: Review of Units I, II, III and IV
 II. Purpose: To review and refresh the important concepts of Units I, II, III and IV.
III. Materials
    A. Teacher materials
        1. Final tests on Unit I, Day 11; Unit II, Day 11; Unit III, Day 11; and Unit IV, Day 11
    B. Student materials
        1. Final tests on Unit I, Day 11, page 13; Unit II, Day 11, page 24; Unit III, Day 11, page 35; and Unit IV, Day 11, page 45 in workbook
IV. Sequence of lesson
    A. Teacher activities
        1. Teacher should select important questions from unit tests and thoroughly discuss these with students. Certain questions are more meaningful for review, depending on the needs of students and emphasis of classroom activities and teacher. The best type of review is a free verbal interchange between students and teacher where needed. Seek reinforcing statements from students who are working on a job. This review can be meaningful if the teacher motivates the group.
    B. Student activities
        1. Students discuss meaningful questions.
 V. Summary
Teacher says, "Today we tried to review the important ideas

we had studied in past units. Tomorrow we will review Unit V, which we have studied the past two weeks. The main purpose of these two days of review is to remind you of the important ideas that you should have learned."

UNIT V   DAY 10

Being on Time

 I. Subject: Review of Unit V
 II. Purpose: To review and reinforce concepts presented in Unit V.
III. Materials
   A. Teacher materials: none
   B. Student materials
      1. Workbook, Unit V, Days 1, 2, 3, 4, 6, 7, 8
IV. Sequence of lesson
   A. Teacher activities
      1. The teacher should select important material from Days 1, 2, 3, 4, 6, 7, 8 for review. Obviously, seven days of content is an overabundance of material to present in one day. Therefore, the teacher should select content that is more appropriate to the needs of the class. Often, the best type of review can be initiated by asking the class what they think is important in this unit and reinforcing this material. The teacher should be imaginative in adapting these units to suit the students' and his own preferences.
   B. Student activities
      1. Students review material under the direction of the teacher.
 V. Summary
Teacher says, "Yesterday and today we reviewed the important parts of all the units we have studied. Tomorrow we will have a test on Unit V and some of the material we studied in other units. You should study all five units tonight so you can learn what is important and do well on the test."

UNIT V   DAY 11

Being on Time

   I. Subject: Test on Unit V
  II. Purpose: To test students' grasp of content and materials studied
      in Unit V.
 III. Materials
      A. Teacher materials: none
      B. Student materials
         1. Workbook, Unit V, Day 11, pages 57–60
  IV. Sequence of lesson
      A. Teacher activities
         1. Teacher says, "We are going to have a test today on
            Unit V. You may use your workbooks. Each question on
            the first part has three answers. You decide which an-
            swers are best. Put a line under all the right answers.
            Part 2 has some sentences. If you think the thoughts are
            right, then circle the word Yes. If you think the thoughts
            are not right, then circle the word No. If you finish early,
            do Part 3 for extra credit." (The teacher should take the
            nonreaders aside and read the questions to them and
            have them mark their answers. The unit test is an excel-
            lent learning device and should be utilized as such.)
         2. After test is completed, collect workbooks and grade test.
      B. Student activities
         1. Weekly test on Unit V, "Being on Time."
   V. Summary
      Teacher says, "I will grade your tests tonight and return them
      to you tomorrow. We'll go over the test tomorrow so you will
      know what questions you had wrong and what to study."

UNIT V DAY 11

Test on Unit V

(Workbook pages 57–60)

Name—————————————————— Date——————————

Part 1

Pick the right answers. Put a line under the right answers. Some of these have more than one right answer. If they do, put a line under all the right sentences.

1. If you have to be on your job by eight o'clock and must change clothes before you start working, how much earlier should you get to the place you work?
   A. 5 minutes.
   B. 15 minutes.
   C. 60 minutes.

2. When you are meeting a friend at two o'clock, what time should you be there?
   A. One o'clock.
   B. Two o'clock.
   C. Three o'clock.

3. People who are often late to work will soon
   A. Get more money.
   B. Keep their jobs.
   C. Lose their jobs.

4. If you were an employer, you would want your workers to be
   A. Always on time.
   B. Never late.
   C. Often late.

5. Being late for school and being late on a job are different because
   A. Being late at school can get you fired.
   B. Being late to work can get you fired.
   C. They are the same.

6. Getting up early in the morning gives you
   A. Time to get ready to go to work.
   B. Time to clean up and get ready to go to work.
   C. Time to clean up, eat breakfast, and get ready to go to work.
7. Getting back to your job after lunch is as important as
   A. Sleeping late.
   B. Not being dependable.
   C. Getting to your job on time in the morning.
8. When would it be good to be late for supper?
   A. When you fool around after work.
   B. When your boss asks you to finish some work you started.
   C. Never.
9. An employer is the
   A. Boss.
   B. Man we work for.
   C. Man who pays us money for working for him.
10. When a person you work with is always on time, you can
    A. Depend on him.
    B. Count on him.
    C. Hope that he doesn't get you fired.
11. Who do you think is a better worker?
    A. Bob.
    B. The boss.
    C. Ben.
12. When we are often late to work our boss and people we work
    with will think that
    A. We don't care for our job.
    B. They can depend on us.
    C. We are good workers.
13. A good way to learn to be on time when you do go to work is to
    A. Be on time for school every day.
    B. Be on time when you must be in a certain place at a certain
       time.
    C. Be late when you feel like it.

Part 2

If you think these thoughts are right underline the word Yes.

If you think these thoughts are not right then underline the word No.

Yes   No   1. A good worker comes to work on time.

Yes   No   2. You can depend on a worker who is often late.

Yes   No   3. When you are late often, you put more work on the people you work with.

Yes   No   4. A boss can depend on you if you are often late to your job.

Yes   No   5. A good worker gives himself plenty of time to get to his job early.

Yes   No   6. Bob was a better worker than Ben.

Yes   No   7. You should depend on your mother to wake you up on time every morning.

Yes   No   8. If you were a boss you would give Ben a job before you would give Bob a job.

Yes   No   9. You would like to work with a person who is always late.

Yes   No   10. A cafeteria is a place where people come to eat.

Part 3

Do this part if you have time.

I. Put down the things that an employer would think about a worker who is always on time.
  1. Cares for his job.
  2. Can depend on him.
  3. Cooperates with other workers.
  4. Has good working habits.
  5. Keep him on the job.
  6. Maybe give him a raise in salary.

II. Put down the things that an employer would think about a worker who is always late.
  1. Doesn't care for his job.
  2. Can't be depended on.
  3. Holds up the other workers.
  4. Some of the other workers will become like him.
  5. Better fire him from the job.

UNIT V   DAY 12

Being on Time

I. Subject: Review of test on Unit V
II. Purpose: To give students an opportunity to correct wrong answers and have a correct guide for future reference.
III. Materials
    A. Teacher materials
        1. Blackboard and chalk
    B. Student materials
        1. Workbook, Unit V, Day 11, pages 57–60
        2. Pencil
IV. Sequence of lesson
    A. Teacher activities
        1. Teacher should go over entire test on Unit V. Solicit answers from students, allowing time for students to correct answers. For Part 3, the optional question, solicit the answers and place on the board. Many students will not have answered this question and the information contained in the answer is very important. It basically sums up Units I through V.
        2. Stress that the test on each unit is an excellent way to review each unit and that students should have the correct answers.
    B. Student activities
        1. Students correct wrong answers to Unit V test.
V. Summary
Teacher says, "You should have all the correct answers for this test on Unit V. The main purpose of getting the right answers is so you have correct information to study and review. The next unit we'll be studying is on being a reliable, dependable person."

UNIT VI

Are You Reliable?
Can We Depend on You?

Time Required: Twelve days

I. Introduction

One of the most common causes for losing a job is absenteeism. This is especially true when the employee fails to call or to notify the employer. During our interviews with employers, a complaint often expressed was, "You can't depend on your help nowadays. They don't show up, and when they do you can't get a good day's work out of them." This thought, with some variation of words, was expressed by over half of the forty-five employers interviewed. When the employee was absent and did call, the employer's feelings were somewhat mollified. This work habit of dependability is stressed over and over again in all twelve units. Reliability and dependability are good working traits that should be instilled in any worker, but especially in the retarded.

The teacher will have noticed by now that there are certain basic habits and traits which are repeated continuously. These traits should also be stressed and reinforced in classroom work and in the daily lives of the students. A certain "hammering" effect may be helpful for classroom teachers of the retarded who wish to instill good working habits in their students. Do not be afraid of being repetitious or boring. Much research indicates that the retarded do not learn coincidentally.

123

II. Objectives
    A. Teacher objectives
        1. To develop in students desirable attitudes toward being at work every day.
        2. To develop in students the attitude of calling or telling the employer when they cannot be at work or when an emergency arises.
        3. To develop in teenage retardates the idea that dependability and reliability include doing good work, finishing a job completely, keeping busy all day, and being a cooperative person.
        4. To develop in students the realization that being absent from work often causes the absentee worker's duties to fall upon his fellow workers.
        5. To prepare the student or worker with a correct routine for telephoning when necessary.
    B. Pupil objectives
        1. To acquire the habit of being at school or work every day.
        2. To develop the habit of calling in or telling the teacher or employer when they are to be absent from work or school.
        3. To develop and acquire the habit and attitude that dependability and reliability include doing good work, finishing a task completely, keeping busy all day, and being a cooperative person.
        4. To acquire the concept that being absent from school or work often forces the work upon fellow workers or students.
        5. To provide oneself with correct information for telephoning when necessary.

UNIT VI   DAYS 1 AND 2

Are You Reliable? Can We Depend on You?

 I. Subject: What happens when you are absent?
 II. Purpose
    A. To teach the concept of what happens when someone is absent from work.
    B. To indoctrinate the "unfairness" of being absent; that other people have to do your job that day.
    C. To inculcate the idea that it is almost impossible to replace a worker who is temporarily absent.
 III. Materials
    A. Teacher materials
       1. Blackboard and chalk
    B. Student materials
       1. Workbook, Unit VI, Days 1 and 2, pages 60–62
 IV. Sequence of lesson
    A. Teacher activities
       1. The concepts to be taught will entail two days of activities. On the second day the teacher should reintroduce the work as a continuation of Day 1.
       2. Teacher says, "We have mentioned in past units the idea of being dependable. In this unit we are going to study more about this idea and see how it affects us in school and on a job. We will also use the word reliable. It means the same as dependable.

         "I am going to ask you to answer some questions today and tomorrow about being dependable or reliable in school and in your everyday lives. Then we will compare these with being dependable on a job. How are they different and how are they the same? Start thinking, and let's see what the correct answers are to these questions I have."
    B. Student activities
       1. At conclusion of each day's activities allow students to copy work from board into workbooks.

V. Summary

Teacher says, "For the past two days we have talked about some of the things a boss wants a worker to be. Actually, we have talked about what makes a person a good worker and whether there are any differences between a good worker on a job or in a school. Tomorrow we'll try to put this discussion into a short listing that you can look at and use as a guide to your work in later life or now in school."

UNIT VI   DAY 1

How Dependable Are You?

(Workbook page 60)

What does dependable or reliable mean in our schoolwork (on our jobs)? Being dependable in school (or on our job) means many different things. What are some of these different things that make us reliable?

1. On time, never late.

   Good student: Being on time every day.

   Good worker: Being on time every day.
                   The same, not different.

   Poor student
     or worker: Often late, he makes other people wait for him.

2. At work every day.

   Good student: Being here every day—not being absent for a poor reason.

   Good worker: Being at work every day—not being absent for a poor reason.
                   The same, not different.

   Poor student
     or worker: Absent too often. You cannot depend on him. He is often absent for no reason at all. When he is absent other people must do his work. He doesn't even call or tell the teacher or boss he will be absent.

3. Listens to directions.

Good student: Listens to and follows directions completely.

Good worker: Listens to and follows directions completely. Does not ask stupid questions. He remembers what to do.
The same, not different.

Poor student
or worker: Doesn't listen to or follow directions. He does things wrong. He wastes time and materials in school or on the job.

UNIT VI   DAY 2

(Workbook page 61)

4. Finishes and does a good job.

Good student: Finishes the job. When he's sure he has done his work, he studies or does some other school-work. He keeps busy quietly or helps other students.

Good worker: Finishes the job completely. He makes sure he is completely finished. He keeps working. He doesn't sit down and rest. He works until break time, then gets a drink or goes to the rest room. If he has no more work, he finds more work or helps his fellow workers. He cooperates.
The same, not different.

Poor student
or worker: Doesn't finish his work. He makes poor grades, or gets fired from his job. He likes to sit around and watch the clock until quitting time.

5. Cooperates, helps others.

Good student: Is in school every day. Helps others who need help. If one of his friends can't read well, he helps him or reads for him. They can depend on him every day. They can count on him.

Good worker: He is at work every day on time. He is co-operative with his fellow workers. He keeps

on working all day. He keeps busy. He co-operates and helps his fellow workers.
The same, not different.

Poor student
or worker: He's often late or absent. When he is late or absent, other workers have to do his work. He is unfair. You cannot depend on him.

6. Is a quiet person.
Good student: Talks in a nice, quiet way. Doesn't make loud noises. Keeps away from bad people.
Good worker: Is a quiet person. Listens carefully to what he is told to do. Doesn't fool around on the job. Comes to work and works with his hands and not with his mouth.

Poor student
or worker: Is a loud person. Talks too much. Fools around and wastes time and material. Not respected by his fellow workers or students.

UNIT VI   DAY 3

Are You Reliable? Can We Depend on You?

 I. Subject: What makes you a good worker?
 II. Purpose: To review and reinforce the personality traits of a successful worker.
 III. Materials
   A. Teacher materials
     1. Blackboard and chalk
   B. Student materials
     1. Workbook, Unit VI, Day 3, page 63
     2. Pen or pencil
 IV. Sequence of lesson
   A. Teacher activities
     1. The aim of today's lesson is to present in a brief form a listing of personality traits that a successful worker will have.

2. Teacher should elicit the items from the students, re-arranging their responses to match the listing below. Again, the success of this type of presentation depends upon the alerting or motivating technique used by the teacher. Discuss fully each trait listed.

B. Student activities

1. Students should list these traits in their workbooks as they are enumerated and placed on the board.

V. Summary

Teacher says, "These eight ideas we listed on the board and in your workbooks are some of the things we have studied this year. Anyone who can do these things well on a job will be able to keep his job.

"You have probably noticed some new words this week. Tomorrow we shall study the new vocabulary that we will continue to use in this and future units."

UNIT VI   DAY 3

What Makes You a Good Worker?

(Workbook page 63)

1. On time.
2. Never absent.
3. Is dependable or reliable.
4. Cooperates.
5. Finishes his work completely.
6. Listens and follows directions.
7. Keeps busy all day.
8. Keeps quiet and has nice manners.

UNIT VI   DAY 4

Are You Reliable? Can We Depend on You?

I. Subject: New vocabulary
II. Purpose: To teach new vocabulary in Unit VI.

III. Materials
    A. Teacher materials
        1. Blackboard and chalk
    B. Student materials
        1. Workbook, Unit VI, Day 4, pages 63–64
        2. Dictionary
        3. Pencil, extra paper
IV. Sequence of lesson
    A. Teacher activities
        1. Teacher says, "There are ten new words to learn this week." Teacher reads list to students.

1. absent	6. fever
2. reliable	7. death
3. completely	8. die
4. sickness	9. funeral
5. headache	10. truth

    B. Student activities
        1. Teacher says, "Write these ten words on some extra paper and then alphabetize them. Then find these words in your dictionaries and write a simple definition of each word on a sheet of notebook paper. We'll check them later and write them in our workbooks." (Allow ample time for students to list words and definitions. Then elicit answers from students, rephrasing their definitions to correspond to listing shown below.

  V. Summary
Teacher says, "Some of the new words seem to come from a sickroom or doctor's office. Well, they did and they should serve as a guide to some good reasons for being absent from work or school. Tomorrow we'll discuss these words and how they relate to being absent from work or school."

UNIT VI   DAY 4

(Workbook pages 63–64)
    1. Absent: To not be there. When you are absent from school or work, you are not there.

2. Completely: To do something completely is to do something until it is finished, with nothing left over to do.
3. Death: When someone dies, he is dead, and we speak of his death.
4. Die: When a person dies, he is gone forever. We can never see him again, only in our thoughts.
5. Fever: A hot feeling we have when we are really sick. We should go to bed when we have a fever.
6. Funeral: When someone dies, we have a funeral. If the funeral is for a close friend or relative, we should be there.
7. Headache: When someone's head hurts, he has a headache. He can usually take something for it to stop the hurt.
8. Reliable: Dependable. If you are reliable, people can count on you.
9. Sickness: When we don't feel well, we are sick. For a real sickness we go to a doctor or go to bed to get well.
10. Truth: To tell the truth is to tell everything in an honest way, with no changing of anything. We should tell the truth all the time.

UNIT VI   DAY 5

Are You Reliable? Can We Depend on You?

I. Subject: Good reasons for being late or absent
II. Purpose: To develop the concept of having an excellent, bona fide reason for being late or absent.
III. Materials
    A. Teacher materials
        1. Blackboard and chalk
    B. Student materials
        1. Notebook and pencil
        2. Workbook, Unit VI, Day 5, pages 64–65
IV. Sequence of lesson
    A. Teacher activities
        1. Teacher says, "We have studied what happens when you

are late or absent from school or work. There are times
when you must be absent or late. There may be an
emergency and you cannot help it. There are times,
though, when you are absent when you should be at
work or at school. Some people are not dependable or
reliable and are absent without any good reason. Let's
see if we can decide what are good, honest reasons for
being absent from school or work. Let's make a list of
these reasons." (Develop these concepts to suit your own
method of presentation.)

2. Elicit answers from students and rearrange their reasons
to coincide with listing shown below.

V. Summary

Teacher says, "You can see that there are very few honest
reasons for being absent. Luckily these reasons don't happen
very often, which means that we should not be absent very
often. Someone asked the question 'What can you do if you must
be absent and you can't help it?' This is an excellent question
and we'll try to answer it tomorrow."

UNIT VI   DAY 5

Good Reasons for Being Absent from School or Work

(Workbook pages 64–65)

1. Sickness: We mean really sick—not just a light cold or a
headache. If you don't have any fever, you can go to work
most of the time. A lot of people use sickness as a reason for
staying home when they are lazy.
2. Very important business: Sometimes we must take care of very
important business. Most of the time it only takes a little time.
We can go to work, go take care of our business, and then go
back to work.
3. Death in the family: When someone in our family dies, we
have to stay home and help the family or go to the funeral.

Most other times when we stay home we are only trying to fool
our boss or teacher. We only fool ourselves, because we know

when we are telling the truth. We cannot fool ourselves and I don't think we can completely fool our boss or teacher.

UNIT VI   DAY 6

Are You Reliable? Can We Depend on You?

 I. Subject: What to do if you must be late or absent
 II. Purpose: To develop in students the steps and techniques to follow when they must be absent or late.
III. Materials
   A. Teacher materials
     1. Blackboard and chalk
   B. Student materials
     1. Workbook, Unit VI, Day 6, pages 65–66
     2. Pencil
IV. Sequence of lesson
   A. Teacher activities
     1. Conscientious people are usually absent or late concomitant with the conditions of knowing beforehand, unexpected illness, or similar situations, or because of an emergency. Basically all three conditions can be handled by notifying the proper party before, during, or immediately after the lateness or absence. The important concept to be taught is proper notification to the authority figure.
     2. Teacher says, "All of us have been absent or late many times. Sometimes we know beforehand if we will be late or absent. Sometimes we don't know and suddenly find out that we can't be at school or work on time or that we must be absent. Let's talk about the reasons for being late or absent and what we should do any time we are late or absent." (Elicit each reason separately, asking what to do about it.)
   B. Student activities
     1. As each concept is developed, allow students to transfer information to their workbooks.

V. Summary

Impress upon your students the need to call or notify their boss or teacher any time they will be late or absent.

UNIT VI   DAY 6

What to Do If You Must Be Late or Absent

(Workbook pages 65–66)

1. Be prepared:

   Keep a small envelope in your pocketbook or wallet with a dime in it just for making a phone call if you need it. Write the name of your boss on the envelope. Write the phone number on the envelope. Use the dime only for calling if you are going to be absent or late. Be smart. Be prepared.

2. If you know before:

   Tell your boss or teacher beforehand. Maybe they can get someone to take your place so your work will not have to be done by your fellow workers. This is the fair thing to do. It shows that you have good manners and think of other people.

3. Can't help it:

   What can you do if suddenly you have to stay home? You get up in the morning and you really are sick and have fever. Call the school or business and ask for your teacher or boss. If they are not there, someone will tell them you called and said you were sick and couldn't come to work or school. This shows a good attitude and that you are thinking of your job. Nothing makes a boss more angry than having one of his workers stay home and not call. Always call your boss or school if you are going to be absent.

4. Suddenly:

   What can you do if suddenly you find that you are going to be late? Let's say that the car or bus you are coming to work in breaks down and you will be late. All you can do is try to call. Sometimes you can't call, but if you can, call and tell them you will be late. Always try to call. This shows that you are thinking of your job and are trying to do the right thing.

UNIT VI   DAY 7

Are You Reliable? Can We Depend on You?

  I. Subject: When can you be late or absent and what should you do?

 II. Purpose: To review and reinforce in brief form the concepts of not being late or absent except under special circumstances, and what to do if one must be late or absent.

III. Materials
    A. Teacher materials
      1. Blackboard and chalk
    B. Student materials
      1. Workbook, Unit VI, Day 7, page 66

IV. Sequence of lesson
    A. Teacher activities
      1. Teacher says, "For the past two days we have discussed the two very important ideas of not being absent or late and what to do if we must be absent or late. Let's review these two ideas and put down the main points to remember."
      2. Solicit the short phrases shown below. Discuss each concept fully. Allow students to list these in their workbooks as each is discussed.

  V. Summary
Teacher says, "Can you see how all the ideas we have learned can help you be more reliable and dependable students? But there are other definitions and meanings for being reliable and dependable. We'll talk about these tomorrow."

UNIT VI   DAY 7

Good Reasons for Being Absent from Work or School

(Workbook page 66)
  1. Real honest sickness.
  2. Very important business.

3. Death in the family (or someone dying).
   Most other times we should go to work. You might fool the boss or teacher, but you cannot fool yourself.

What should you do if you are absent or late?

1. Keep a dime and your boss's name and phone number with you at all times.
2. If you know beforehand, tell your teacher or boss.
3. If it's a sudden sickness, call the school or business.
4. If it's a sudden lateness, always try to call if you can.
   Always call. It shows that you are interested in your job and that you have good manners. Calling shows you have a good attitude.

UNIT VI　DAY 8

Are You Reliable? Can We Depend on You?

I. Subject: Other meanings of reliable and dependable
II. Purpose
   A. To instill the concept of reliability as related to doing work correctly.
   B. To instill the concept of dependability as related to doing a full day's work.
   C. To instill the concept of reliability as related to completing the work.
   D. To instill the concept of dependability as related to fellow workers.
III. Materials
   A. Teacher materials: none
   B. Student materials
      1. Workbook, Unit VI, Day 8, page 67
IV. Sequence of lesson
   A. Teacher activities
      1. Teacher says, "Today's new material is related to some different meanings of dependability and reliability. We have talked about some of the meanings before, but to-day we shall see that dependability and reliability have

some other meanings. What other meanings do you think these two words might have? Put your thinking hats on and tell me what other meanings reliable and dependable have?"

B. Student activities

  1. Students answer and discuss questions asked by teacher. After each question, teacher places answers on board and students copy them into their workbooks.

V. Summary

Teacher says, "You can see that reliable and dependable have other important meanings besides being on time and at work every day. It is important to be reliable and dependable after you get to work. Tomorrow we'll combine all the meanings and definitions of reliable and dependable and see how you rate on them. We'll add some of the rating forms from other units and compare them to past scores you made."

UNIT VI DAY 8

Some Other Meanings of Dependable and Reliable

(Workbook page 67)

  1. Do good work.

    Is the kind of work you do dependable? When you finish your work, does someone have to do it over again? Is it the best you can do and is it as good as your fellow workers'? If it has to be done over, then you are not a dependable worker.

  2. Complete your work.

    Do you finish your work? Does someone else have to finish it for you? Can your boss depend on you to finish the job completely with no leftovers?

  3. Keep working.

    Do you give your boss a full day's work? Do you give him back in a good day's work what he pays you in salary? Do you give him some extras? In school your salary is your grades. If your grades are poor, then you are not working hard. Get the habit of working hard in school and you will carry this habit to your jobs when you finish school.

4. Cooperate.

Are you dependable and reliable with your fellow workers? Do you do your work and a little extra? Can they count on you all the time? If they need your help, do you give it willingly? This makes them respect you.

UNIT VI   DAY 9

Are You Reliable? Can We Depend on You?

I. Subject: How dependable a worker are you? Rate yourself.
II. Purpose: To reinforce concepts taught in units by allowing students to rate themselves.
III. Materials
    A. Teacher materials: none
    B. Student materials
        1. Workbook, Unit VI, Day 9, page 68
        2. Pencil
IV. Sequence of lesson
    A. Teacher activities
        1. The important concepts of Unit VI have been arranged into a rating scale. Read each item and allow students to rate themselves. At conclusion of rating, allow each student to add his own scores and divide by the number of items. Teacher should take all scores and derive a mean. Then explain students' scores and their class standing in relation to the mean.
        2. Teacher says, "In your workbook, Unit VI, Day 9 on page 68, you will find a rating scale. I will read each item and you score yourself."
V. Summary

Teacher says, "Look at how you rated yourself. Where were your scores low? Where were they high? Work on improving your low scores. One low score on a job can get you fired. Ask me or your friends what you can do to become a better worker and person. Tomorrow we will review this unit and get ready for our unit test."

How dependable a worker are you? Rate yourself: Am I Doing Better?

Things I Am and Things I Do:	Always 5	Most of the time 4	Sometimes 3	Once in a while 2	Never 1
1. On time	✓				
2. Come to school	✓				
3. Dependable		✓			
4. Cooperate		✓			
5. Finish the job	✓				
6. Listen and follow directions		✓			
7. Keep busy all day	✓				
8. Am quiet and have nice manners	✓				
9. Do good work	✓				
10. Do a full honest day's work	✓				
11. Help others	✓				
12. Good personality	✓				
13. Have a good attitude	✓				
MY SCORE:					

UNIT VI   DAY 10

Are You Reliable? Can We Depend on You?

  I. Subject: Review of Unit VI
 II. Purpose: To review and reinforce pertinent information in Unit
     VI.
III. Materials
    A. Teacher materials: none
    B. Student materials
      1. Workbook, Unit VI, Days 3, 7 and 8
 IV. Sequence of lesson
    A. Teacher activities
      1. The pertinent information in Unit VI is contained in
         Days 3, 7 and 8. The teacher should review these days,
         using the format shown on each day. Discuss fully each
         day's information. Ask questions concerning the materials
         and answer all pertinent questions posed by students.
  V. Summary
    Teacher says, "We have tried to review the important informa-
tion contained in this unit. Tomorrow we will have a test on
Unit VI. Study the entire unit tonight. If you cannot read the
unit yourself, ask someone in your family to read it for you."

UNIT VI   DAY 11

Are You Reliable? Can We Depend on You?

  I. Subject: Test on Unit VI
 II. Purpose: To test students' grasp of Unit VI.
III. Materials
    A. Teacher materials: none
    B. Student materials
      1. Workbook, Unit VI, Day 11, pages 69–70
      2. Pencil

IV. Sequence of lesson
  A. Teacher activities
    1. Teacher says, "Today we are having our unit test. If you studied hard and did your work well, you should make a good grade. Let's read the instructions." (Read to class the written instructions for all three parts.)

UNIT VI   DAY 11

Test on Unit VI

(Workbook pages 69–70)

Name———————————————— Date————————————

Part 1

Put the right word into each sentence. There are 12 words and only 10 sentences. This means that you will have 2 words left over.

1.	truth	7.	certain
2.	funeral	8.	personality
3.	die	9.	sick
4.	absent	10.	fever
5.	reliable	11.	death
6.	completed	12.	headache

1. When your head hurts, you have a headache.
2. When you are not at work or school, you are absent.
3. When you tell everything right and don't change anything, you are telling the truth.
4. When a person dies, there is always a funeral.
5. When you don't feel well and have a fever, you are sick.
6. Death and to die mean the same thing.
7. A person you can depend on is a reliable person.
8. When you are sick and feel hot, you have a fever and should go to bed.
9. A good honest reason to stay home from work or school is a death in the family.
10. When you have done something well and there are no leftovers to finish, you have completed the job.

Part 2

If you think the sentence is right underline the Yes. If you think the sentence is wrong underline the No.

Yes No   1. A reliable person is often late.
Yes No   2. A dependable person is at work or school every day.
Yes No   3. A reliable person does his work and some extra work.
Yes No   4. A dependable person listens, remembers and follows directions so he can waste material and time.
Yes No   5. You can get into good work habits in school and carry them over to your job.
Yes No   6. A good reason for being absent is a headache.
Yes No   7. You can fool other people, but you cannot fool yourself. You can only tell the truth to yourself.
Yes No   8. If you are going to be absent from work or school, never call your teacher or boss.
Yes No   9. If you are suddenly late for work or school, try to call your teacher or boss.
Yes No 10. When you call your boss or teacher when you must be absent or late, it shows that you don't care about your job and that you have a poor attitude.
Yes No 11. A dependable worker does good work and no one has to do it over.
Yes No 12. A reliable worker can be counted on to do his work, to cooperate with his fellow workers, and to do extra work.
Yes No 13. A willing worker never helps his fellow workers.
Yes No 14. A dependable worker works hard all day long and does not sit around.
Yes No 15. When you are a dependable worker, people will not respect you.

Part 3

Extra credit: If you get part of this right or all of it right, you earn extra credit. If you get it wrong, nothing will be taken off your grade.
1. What are the 13 things we listed that show you are a reliable, dependable worker?
   1. On time.

2. Never absent.
3. Dependable.
4. Cooperates.
5. Finishes job.
6. Listens and follows directions.
7. Keeps busy all day.
8. Is quiet, has nice manners.
9. Does good work.
10. Is honest in his work.
11. Helps others.
12. Good personality.
13. Good attitude.

UNIT VI   DAY 12

Are You Reliable? Can We Depend on You?

I. Subject: Review of test on Unit VI
II. Purpose
   A. To review and reinforce information taught in Unit VI.
   B. To allow students to correct wrong answers so they will have a correct guide to study and use in later years.
III. Materials
   A. Teacher materials: none
   B. Student materials
      1. Workbook, Unit VI, Day 11, pages 69–70
      2. Pencil
IV. Sequence of lesson
   A. Teacher activities
      1. Teacher should read all questions and allow sufficient time for students to correct wrong answers. Whenever a disproportionate number of students have answered a question incorrectly, spend extra time on this question, making sure that students understand the concept involved.
V. Summary
Teacher says, "Our next unit is on honesty. We will start this tomorrow."

UNIT VII

Honesty Is Still the Best

Time Required: Twelve days

I. Introduction

Dishonesty is one of the reasons for which an employee will be most promptly discharged from a job. Virtually no employer will allow pilfering or stealing on the part of his workers. Of the forty-five employers interviewed, forty-two stated that they would discharge an employee for stealing. The other three employers were in the type of business where there was no possibility of stealing. Related to this question was the understanding by employers that their employees could consume anything made in the business on the premises, but that they could not remove any product from the premises.

Several employers who were in wholesale jobbing or in small manufacturing businesses, where consumer items were sold or made, stated that they were now using professional agencies to stop stealing. Virtually all of these agencies employed lie-detector equipment. None of the employers had discontinued the use of this lie-detecting equipment after its introduction, and many stated that their inventory controls showed an almost complete stoppage of stealing after the initial and continued use of such equipment. None of these employers would hire a new employee unless he had undergone a lie-detecting test. After the new employee was hired, he took periodic lie-detecting tests. It appeared that the use of lie-detecting equipment virtually halted all stealing of this nature.

145

Knowledge of this lie-detection technique should be part of the educable mentally retarded student's background. Of greater importance is the employee's attitude and how he values honesty. An honest person has nothing to fear from any lie-detection techniques. If the value of honesty can be made part of the personality structure of the retarded, there is no doubt that he will be a better functioning member of the socioeconomic world.

II. Objectives
  A. Teacher objectives
    1. To develop the desirable value of honesty and all its ramifications.
    2. To develop the desirable value of truthfulness.
    3. To develop a model of honest interaction in school and on the job.
    4. To review some of the other connotations of honesty.
    5. To provide some background on a lie-detection test.
  B. Pupil objectives
    1. To acquire the value of honesty and all its ramifications.
    2. To acquire the value of truthfulness.
    3. To acquire a model of honesty.
    4. To review some of the other connotations of honesty.
    5. To gain some background about a lie-detection test.

UNIT VII   DAYS 1 AND 2

Honesty Is Still the Best

I. Subject: Honesty in school and on the job
II. Purpose
  A. To teach or give the student a many-sided definition of honesty in school and in job situations.
  B. To indoctrinate the value of honesty as related to stealing in school and job situations.
  C. To instill the value of honesty as related to the taking of extra time or breaks, lateness, or lunchtime in school and on the job.

D. To teach the value of truthfulness at all times.

E. To review other facets of honesty.

III. Materials

    A. Teacher materials

        1. Blackboard and chalk

    B. Student materials

        1. Workbook, Unit VII, Days 1 and 2, pages 71–72

IV. Sequence of lesson

    A. Teacher activities

        1. Teacher says, "All of us are honest. Some of us are more honest than others. Each one of us has a little different attitude toward honesty. Some of us think it's right to keep a pen we find on the floor or outside. Some of us think it should be turned in to the lost-and-found room or given to the teacher. It is hard to say which one is right or wrong. Your attitude toward honesty depends a lot on what your families think about honesty. What we are going to do today is to put our attitudes toward honesty on the board and then we will have something that we can go by. First, let's see how we all feel about honesty in school." (Ask the following questions and write answers as shown below. Leave space below school listing for work listing.)

    B. Student activities

    1. Allow students sufficient time to copy information from board into their workbooks.

V. Summary

    A. Throughout two days of classwork the teacher should stress the concept that honesty is a personal trait which a person must develop in himself.

    B. Teacher says, "There are other meanings to honesty than these that we have talked about. Let's stop here because we don't have enough time to go over the other meanings. Tomorrow we'll continue with more discussion about honesty."

UNIT VII   DAY 1

Honesty in School and Job

(Workbook page 71)

What do we mean by honesty in school (or job)?

Good worker
or student   1. No stealing of anything.
                   No difference, the same.

Poor worker
or student   1. Steals things that belong to other people.

Good worker
or student   2. No cheating on tests or someone else's work.
                   No difference, the same.

Poor worker
or student   2. Cheats on tests or cheats on his work.

Good worker
or student   3. No cheating on time during school or job,
                   breaks or lunch.
                   No difference, the same.

Poor worker
or student   3. Cheats on his time during work, or breaks, or
                   lunch. Takes some extra minutes away from the
                   boss's time.
                   This is stealing the boss's time.

UNIT VII   DAY 2

Honesty in School and Job

(Workbook pages 71–72)

Good worker
or student   4. Telling the truth at all times.
                   No difference, the same.

Poor worker
or student   4. Lies about many things, being absent or late, or about answering questions. He is not reliable.

Good worker
or student   5. He pays his debts.
No difference, the same.

Poor worker
or student   5. He always owes money. He doesn't pay his debts. You cannot rely on him to keep his word.

An honest person does these things in school or on a job:
1. Never steals or cheats on anything or at any time.
2. Always tells the truth.
3. Always pays his debts and keeps his word.
4. Knows that the only person who can keep him honest is himself.

UNIT VII   DAYS 3 AND 4

Honesty Is Still the Best

I. Subject: How to be honest
II. Purpose
  A. To teach a model of honest behavior.
  B. Review Unit VII, Days 1 and 2
III. Materials
  A. Teacher material: none
  B. Student materials
    1. Workbook, Unit VII, Days 1, 2, 3 and 4
IV. Sequence of lesson
  A. Teacher activities
    1. Teacher says, "Let's reread Days 1 and 2 in our workbooks, pages 71–72." (Stress important facts.)
    2. "Today and tomorrow I want to ask some questions that have to do with the last two days' work. We know what

an honest person is. Now the question is, how can you be honest? I'm going to ask you these questions and I want you to answer them. Start thinking."

   B. Student activities
      1. After each question (see below) is discussed and written on the board, students should copy this material into their workbooks, pages 72–74.

V. Summary
   A. Again stress that honesty is a personal thing that each person must develop within himself.
   B. Teacher says, "Tomorrow we'll have a few new words to learn. Read them over tonight. They are listed in Day 5, pages 74–75, in your workbook."

UNIT VII   DAY 3

How to Be Honest

(Workbook pages 72–73)

  1. If you find a pen or a tool on the floor or outside on the grounds, what should you do with it?
     Answer: Take it to the lost-and-found room or give it to the teacher or your boss.
     Why?   Just because you find something, that does not make it yours. If you take it back, the person who lost it can ask for it. This is the honest way.

  2. If you see a pocketbook lying on the table and no one is around, what should you do?
     Answer: Leave it alone, or take it to the teacher or boss.
     Why?   Maybe the person who owns it will come back for it. If he left it there and doesn't come back, the honest thing is to take it to your teacher or your boss.

  3. If you are taking a test and your neighbor starts to cheat, what should you do?
     Answer: Cover your paper.
     Why?   Cheating is like stealing. Everyone can study and should do his own work.

UNIT VII   DAY 4

(Workbook pages 73–74)

4. If you have a 30-minute lunchtime, how much time should you take?

   Answer: 30 minutes, no more.

   Why?   If you take longer, you are cheating your boss out of time that he pays you for. It's just like stealing his money.

5. When you are asked a question that is hard to answer truthfully, what should you do?

   Answer: Always answer truthfully.

   Why?   Telling a lie is the same as cheating. You can lie to your boss or teacher, but you cannot lie to yourself.

6. If you owe money to someone and you are supposed to pay on a certain day, what should you do?

   Answer: Pay up your debts on that day.

   Why?   You gave your word to pay. Do it. This is the honest thing to do.

7. Who decides for you that you should do the things we talked about for the past two days?

   Answer: You, yourself, most of the time.

   Why?   Most of the time there is no one around to check up on your honesty. The only policeman around is yourself.

UNIT VII   DAY 5

Honesty Is Still the Best

   I. Subject: New vocabulary
  II. Purpose: To teach students new vocabulary used in this and subsequent units.
 III. Materials
  A. Teacher materials: none
  B. Student materials
     1. Workbook, Unit VII, Day 5, pages 74–75

     2. Dictionary

     3. Pencil and extra paper

IV. Sequence of lesson

   A. Teacher activities

     1. Teacher says, "Today we have five new words to learn. They are: stealing, cheating, debts, safe, lie detector." (Write words on board.) "I want you to write them on some paper and alphabetize them and then write a definition of each in your own words." (Allow students ample time to execute assignment.) "Now we'll go over them on the board and you can copy them in your workbooks."

     2. Place alphabetized list on board and solicit definitions from students. Reword definitions to match listing below. Explain each word fully. After listing on board is complete, have students copy corrected list into workbooks.

   B. Student activities

     1. Students will look up words in dictionary and write simple definitions.

 V. Summary

Teacher says, "Tomorrow we are going to discuss lie-detector tests and how they are used in businesses."

UNIT VII DAY 5

(Workbook pages 74–75)

   1. Cheating: To take something that is not yours. Sometimes we cheat when we steal answers from a neighbor's paper.

   2. Debts: When you owe money, you have a debt. When you give your word to do something that is like a debt. Always pay your debts on time.

   3. Lie detector: A machine that can tell if you have lied or cheated, or stolen something, or if you are telling the truth.

   4. Safe: To be safe is to do something right so you won't get hurt. To do the right thing is the safe thing.

   5. Stealing: To take something that is not yours.

UNIT VII   DAY 6

Honesty Is Still the Best

I. Subject: What is a lie-detector test?

II. Purpose: To enable students to understand what a lie-detector test is, and why a person cannot lie or cheat on this test.

III. Materials

   A. Teacher materials

   1. Blackboard and chalk

   B. Student materials

   1. Workbook, Unit VII, Day 6, page 76

IV. Sequence of lesson

   A. Teacher activities

   1. Teacher says, "Many businesses find that their employees are stealing time and material from the businesses. This loss amounts to a great deal of money. Many businesses have gone under because they were not able to stand these losses. Owners of businesses have had to find some way to stop this stealing from their businesses. They did find a way, and it is called a lie-detector test. Many of you will be taking this test when you finish school and go looking for jobs. The important thing to remember is that an honest person has nothing to be afraid of when he takes this test. This test can tell if you are lying or telling the truth. In your workbooks on page 76 is a description of how a lie-detector test is done and why it is used. Let's read this together and discuss it."

   2. At each step of the lie-detector test, explain fully the procedure and answer any questions the class has. Impress upon the students that there is no danger or pain attached to taking a lie-detector test.

   B. Student activities

   1. Students read the description of the lie-detector test with the teacher, Unit VII, Day 6, page 76.

V. Summary

Teacher says, "If you ever have to take a lie-detector test you'll know what it's all about. Actually, it's a very simple thing and there is no danger or pain at all. Tomorrow we are going to look at how our work habits have become better or worse since we started studying these units."

The Lie-Detector Test

1. You go to look for a job. If your boss wants to employ you, he will tell you to go to a certain place to take a lie-detector test.
2. You go there and they sit you down at a table. They will put a round piece of rubber on your arm and body. It does not hurt at all.
3. They will ask you some easy questions like "What is your name?" or "Where do you live?"
4. The man has a place to read on the machine when you answer the questions. He can tell if you are lying or telling the truth. Always tell the truth.
5. Then he asks you questions like "Have you ever stolen anything?" or "Would you cheat or steal if you had a chance?" When you answer, he will know if you are lying or telling the truth. Always tell the truth.
6. The man tells your boss if you are honest. After you are hired for the job, you will have to go back every once in a while for more tests.
7. When you go back for more tests after you have worked in the business for some time, they will find out if you have stolen from them or cheated the business since the last test. If you are honest and do not cheat or steal, you will keep your job. You cannot fool the machine.
8. You can start out being honest and pass your first lie-detector tests. If you steal between tests, the machine will find it out when you take your next test and you will lose your job. You cannot fool the machine.

UNIT VII   DAY 7

Honesty Is Still the Best

I. Subject: Let's rate ourselves
II. Purpose
   A. Review of concepts studied in Units I, III and IV.
   B. To determine whether students' perception of their behavior as measured by rating scales in Units I, III and IV has changed from original rating.

III. Materials
    A. Teacher materials: none
    B. Student materials
        1. Workbook, Unit VII, Day 7, pages 77–79
IV. Sequence of lesson
    A. Teacher activities
        1. Teacher says, "Today we are going to rate ourselves on whether we have changed our work habits since we started studying these units. Turn to page 77 in your workbook and we'll read these together and you rate yourself."
        2. Teacher should explain rating system. Read all items to students, allowing them sufficient time to mark their rating forms.
        3. At conclusion of ratings, have students add up their scores and divide by number of items. Do this separately for each rating scale.
        4. Have students compare scores on original rating scale, Unit I, page 8; Unit III, page 34; Unit IV, page 44. Teacher should also make note of original and new scores. This could be an indication of students' perception of their own behavior, and whether the concepts being taught in the units are beginning to shape students' behavior.
    B. Student activities
        1. Students rate their own forms, and compile scores.
V. Summary
Teacher says, "By comparing the rating scales in Units I, III and IV with today's rating scale, you can see how you have improved or become worse in your working habits. Again look for your low scores and think about what you can do to make them better. If you don't know what to do to improve, let's talk it over together. Maybe both of us can think of some ideas that could help you. Tomorrow we're going to read a story about our two girl friends, Ginger and Jane."

Self-Rating Scale: Am I Doing Better?

Things I Do:	Always 5	Most of the time 4	Sometimes 3	Once in a while 2	Never 1
1. Come on time					
2. Come every day					
3. Do my work					
4. Never talk back					
5. Ask for help					
6. Get along					
7. Try to be a good worker					
8. Do my best					
MY SCORE:					

Self-Rating Scale

Things I Do:	Always 5	Most of the time 4	Sometimes 3	Once in a while 2	Never 1
1. Try hard; am not lazy; am a good worker					
2. Listen and follow directions; ask good questions					
3. Get along; cooperate; help out when asked					
4. Finish the job; start a job and finish it					
5. Am willing to be told what to do; don't talk back					
6. Am interested in the work; try to do well					
7. Like my job and the people around me					
8. Come on time every day; am never late					
9. Am willing to stay late and finish the job					
10. Keep busy and keep on working					
11. Do extra work without being asked					
12. Am honest; do a full day's work and never take anything home					
MY SCORE:					

Self-Rating Scale

Things I Do:	Always 5	Most of the time 4	Sometimes 3	Once in a while 2	Never 1
1. Listen carefully to directions					
2. Remember directions					
3. Ask good questions if I'm not sure					
4. Do not waste my time					
5. Do not waste material					
6. Do not waste other people's time					
7. Have good working habits					
8. Find more work when I'm finished					
9. Keep busy					
10. Do not rest except at break time					
11. Finish a job all the way					
12. Work hard					
13. Cooperate and help other people					
14. Am dependable; come to work every day					
15. Am respected by other people					
16. Am on time every day					
MY SCORE:					

UNIT VII   DAY 8

Honesty Is Still the Best

I. Subject: Story "Jane Gets Fired for Stealing"
II. Purpose: To review all concepts of honesty covered in this unit in the form of a story about Ginger and Jane.
III. Materials
    A. Teacher materials: none
    B. Student materials
        1. Workbook, Unit VII, Day 8, page 80
IV. Sequence of lesson
    A. Teacher activities
        1. Teacher says, "Our new material for today is a story about Ginger and Jane. In this story Jane . . . well, let's see what happened to Jane. Remember our last story about these two girls? Ginger is the nice girl and Jane is the foolish girl."
        2. While reading the story with students, emphasize and discuss the portions of the story pertinent to honesty. Stress the concept that Ginger was honest and Jane dishonest because they themselves wanted to be this way.
    B. Student activities
        1. Students read story with teacher.
V. Summary
Teacher says, "This is a true story and it happens many times. One thing any employer will never allow is cheating or stealing. It's the fastest way to get fired from a job. Tomorrow we'll try to decide why Jane was fired and Ginger was respected."

Jane Gets Fired for Stealing

Ginger and Jane were still working at the cleaning plant. Ginger was doing well on her job. She was honest and a good worker. Whenever she found any money or anything in the clothes she cleaned, she would turn it in to her boss. Her fellow workers knew that Ginger would never take anything that belonged to someone else. She was truthful and reliable. They could depend on her honesty. She was a nice, honest girl.

Jane also worked on the clothes before they went into the cleaning machine. When Jane would find money in the clothes, she would keep it. One time she found a small pocketbook in a dress with a lot of money in it. She kept the money and threw away the pocketbook. When she found a pin on a dress, she would take it home and keep it. Many times her boss would ask the girls if they had found certain things that had been left in the clothes. She would say no. The other girls knew that Jane had found some of these things. They didn't like to think that the boss thought that maybe some of them had stolen these things. They didn't like Jane because she was a cheat and stole things. One day the boss asked all the girls to take a lie-detector test. Too many things were missing. Each girl had to go into a room and take the test. All of them did well on the test but Jane. She tried to lie and said that she had never taken anything. She couldn't lie to the lie-detector machine. It caught her. The boss was real nice and he only fired her. He could have turned her over to the police but he didn't. Everyone was glad to see her fired. No one respected her. After that, the boss didn't have to ask the girls about missing things. They all passed the test and he knew that they were honest.

UNIT VII   DAY 9

Honesty Is Still the Best

I. Subject: Which one are you: Ginger or Jane?
II. Purpose: To review the important concepts of honesty presented in story form.
III. Materials
    A. Teacher materials: none
    B. Student materials
        1. Workbook, Unit VII, Days 8 and 9, pages 80–81
        2. Pencil
IV. Sequence of lesson
    A. Teacher activities
        1. Teacher says, "Yesterday we read a story about Ginger and Jane. Jane lost her job, and Ginger kept her job and was respected by her employer and fellow workers. Let's

read the story again and see if we can list on the board why Jane was fired and why Ginger kept her job."

    2. Teacher and students read story. As story is read, teacher should emphasize facts shown below. Discuss each concept fully and stress that honesty is a personal trait. As listing is made, allow students to copy information into their workbooks.

  B. Student activities

    1. Students copy information into their workbooks as listing is made on the board.

V. Summary

Teacher says, "We listed all the things that Ginger and Jane did to show their honesty or dishonesty. But the important idea to remember is that it was up to Ginger and Jane themselves to decide what they should do. It's the same thing with you. Each of you, yourselves, has to decide whether you will be honest or dishonest. Tomorrow we'll review this unit and have our test the day after."

UNIT VII   DAY 9

(Workbook pages 80–81)

Why Ginger kept her job: She	Why Jane lost her job: She
1. was honest.	1. was dishonest.
2. never stole.	2. stole a lot of things.
3. never cheated.	3. cheated a lot.
4. turned in to the boss things that didn't belong to her.	4. kept things that didn't belong to her.

Who watched Ginger and kept her honest?

No one except Ginger. She wanted to be honest and no one had to watch her.

Who caused Jane to cheat and steal?

No one but Jane. No one cheats or steals unless he himself wants to.

UNIT VII   DAY 10

Honesty Is Still the Best

   I. Subject: Review of Unit VII
  II. Purpose: To review material presented in Unit VII.
 III. Materials
     A. Teacher materials: none
     B. Student materials
       1. Workbook, Unit VII, Days 3, 4 and 7
  IV. Sequence of lesson
     A. Teacher activities
       1. Teacher should review the days noted. Carefully discuss any questions. Use format shown in each day's lessons. This review day can be an excellent method of fusing the important concepts into a "whole." Allow time for students to ask questions concerning any part of the unit they need help on.
     B. Student activities
       1. Students review and discuss the lesson on honesty with teacher.
   V. Summary
   Teacher says, "Tomorrow we will have our test on Unit VII. Tonight study your workbook."

UNIT VII   DAY 11

Honesty Is Still the Best

   I. Subject: Test on Unit VII
  II. Purpose: To test students' grasp of material taught in this unit.
 III. Materials
     A. Teacher materials: none
     B. Student materials

      1. Pencil
      2. Workbook, Unit VII, Day 11, pages 81–83
IV. Sequence of lesson
   A. Teacher activities
      1. Teacher says, "We are having our unit test today. Let's read the instructions on all three parts. [Read instructions as shown on test papers.] You may use your workbooks."

UNIT VII DAY 11

Test on Unit VII

(Workbook pages 81–83)

Name_____ Date_____

Part 1

Pick the right answers to these sentences. If there is more than one answer, then pick all the right answers.
1. An honest person
   A. Steals
   B. Cheats
   C. Never takes anything that doesn't belong to him
2. Cheating on a test is
   A. Honest
   B. Dishonest
   C. Like stealing
3. If you have a 30-minute lunchtime and you take only 30 minutes, you are
   A. Honest
   B. Reliable
   C. Stealing time
4. A person who lies is a
   A. Cheat
   B. Honest person

C. Person who doesn't keep his word
5. Honest people
    A. Never keep their word
    B. Pay their debts
    C. Keep their word
6. If you find some money on the floor, you should
    A. Give it to the teacher
    B. Take it to the lost-and-found room
    C. Keep it
7. Telling a lie is like
    A. Honesty
    B. Cheating
    C. Stealing
8. Being truthful is what an
    A. Undependable person does
    B. Unreliable person does
    C. Honest person does
9. When you lie you can
    A. Fool the person you are lying to
    B. Fool yourself
    C. Not fool yourself
10. You cannot lie to
    A. Yourself
    B. Other people
    C. A lie-detector machine

Part 2

If the sentence is right put a line under the Yes. If the sentence is wrong put a line under the No.

Yes No   1. Jane was an honest person.
Yes No   2. Stealing time from your boss is dishonest.
Yes No   3. Not paying debts is honest.
Yes No   4. When you give your word, you must keep it.
Yes No   5. A lie-detector machine can tell if you are honest.
Yes No   6. An honest person does not have to be afraid of a lie-detecting test.
Yes No   7. You can fool a lie-detecting machine.

Yes No 8. Ginger never took anything that did not belong to her.

Yes No 9. Jane was not respected by her fellow workers.

Yes No 10. Jane's boss was right when he fired her.

Part 3

Extra Credit

1. List the things that make a person honest.
   1. Never steals.
   2. Always tells the truth.
   3. On time every day.
   4. Is dependable and reliable.
   5. Does his job.
   6. Wants to be honest.

UNIT VII   DAY 12

Honesty Is Still the Best

I. Subject: Review and correction of unit test
II. Purpose
   A. To review information in Unit VII.
   B. To allow students to correct test on Unit VII so they will have a correct study guide for future reference.
III. Materials
   A. Teacher materials: none
   B. Student materials
      1. Workbook, Unit VII, Day 11, pages 81–83
      2. Pencil
IV. Sequence of lesson
   A. Teacher activities
      1. Teacher should go over each question, explaining the correct answers. If there were a large number of specific questions incorrectly answered, give extra time to these questions. Allow time for students to correct wrong answers.

B. Student activities
1. Students review test with teacher and correct wrong answers.

V. Summary

Teacher says, "The most important idea in this unit is that it is up to each person himself to be honest. No person or test can force you to be honest except you yourself. Our next unit will be on working harder for a raise in salary or grades."

UNIT VIII

How to Get a Raise in Salary

Time required: Twelve days

I. Introduction

Many retarded workers have a lackadaisical attitude toward bettering themselves. They are content to hold a job at a constant level and often are unmotivated toward self-improvement. Their attitude toward striving for higher-level job performance is often lethargic. Many times a retarded worker is fired from a job he is doing adequately because the employer sees no possibility of his ever functioning at a higher level and rising above his present position. As one employer aptly said, "I've got plenty of average help. I need some eager beavers." He continued, "I want people who will produce more, who can work their way up, who will give this business that something extra that makes for a successful business." If this attitude of continuing to improve and to produce more can be instilled into the value system of a retarded worker, it will aid his chances of being a successful job-holder.

II. Objectives

A. Teacher objectives

1. To develop in students desirable attitudes toward improving their technical and social skills and gaining advancement.

167

2. To inculcate in students information concerning some techniques for obtaining a raise in salary.
3. To explain how and why a worker can improve himself and advance in job status and salary.
B. Student objectives
   1. To acquire desirable attitudes and motivation toward improving technical and social skills.
   2. To develop an understanding of the ramifications involved in obtaining a raise in salary or grades.
   3. To develop feasible techniques for improving job and social skills.

UNIT VIII   DAY 1

How to Get a Raise in Salary

  I. Subject: What is a raise in salary or grades?
 II. Purpose: To define a raise in salary or grades.
III. Materials needed
   A. Teacher materials
      1. Blackboard and chalk
   B. Student materials
      1. Workbook, Unit VIII, Day 1, page 83
      2. Pen or pencil
 IV. Sequence of lesson
   A. Teacher activities
      1. Teacher says, "In this unit we are going to study about raises in salary or grades. Today we're going to find out what a raise in salary or grades means. Later on we will compare raises in salary on a job and raises in grades in school to see the differences or to see if they are the same. Let's see what you think a raise in salary or grades means? You tell the class what you think it is and I'll list them on the board."
   B. Student activities
      1. Ask each question, and as students respond, write answers on board to correspond to wording below. Discuss

each answer. Have students copy answers into their workbooks.

V. Summary

Teacher says, "Tomorrow we will compare the differences in getting a raise in salary on a job and a raise in grades in school."

UNIT VIII   DAY 1

(Workbook page 83)

1. What does a raise in salary mean?

   Answer: To get more money for the work you do. If you are working for $ .50 an hour on a 40-hour week, how much salary do you make? $20.00 a week. If your boss raises your salary to $ .60 an hour, how much salary would you make a week? $24.00 a week. How much of a raise did you get? $4.00 a week.

2. What does a raise in grades mean?

   Answer: To get higher grades for your schoolwork. If you are making a poor grade in your work, you can work harder, study more, and do extra work and get a better grade. If you are making a D in this course, you can work harder and raise your grade to a C or even a B.

3. Can you get a raise without getting any more money in your salary?

   Answer: Yes. Getting more happiness out of your job is like a raise. You don't get any more money but you are a happier and better person. That can mean a lot to you.

4. Do you know of anyone who works hard 7 days a week and does not get any salary at all? (You girls can tell me this answer better than the boys can.)

   Answer: Yes, your mothers do. They work real hard at home, keeping house, cleaning, washing and cooking. They don't get any salary in money, do they? But the love they have for their families is their salary. Don't you think that doing a better job for their families makes them happier persons?

So you can see that most times a raise in salary means more money. Sometimes a raise only means more happiness. In all kinds of jobs, doing your best and working harder will often give you a raise in salary and almost always give you a raise in happiness and make you a better worker.

UNIT VIII   DAYS 2 AND 3

How to Get a Raise in Salary

   I. Subject: Comparing raises in salary with raises in grades
  II. Purpose
     A. To compare raises in salary and grades.
     B. To enable students to conceptualize that the same effort is required for raises both in school and on a job.
 III. Materials
     A. Teacher materials
        1. Blackboard and chalk
     B. Student materials
        1. Workbook, Unit VIII, Days 2 and 3, pages 84–85
        2. Pencil
 IV. Sequence of lesson
     A. Teacher activities
        1. Presenting this information encompasses two days. At the completion of Day 1, the teacher should say, "Tomorrow we will continue these comparisons. We did not have time to finish listing all your ideas."
        2. Teacher says, "For the next two days we are going to study whether there are any differences in getting a raise in salary on a job or a raise in grades in school. Let's start off with seeing what you have to do to get a raise in grades in school and whether this would be different on a job. All of you go to school so you know what you have to do to raise your grades. We'll list this and see how this would compare to getting a raise in salary on a job. We expect the people who are working

to be able to help us compare and decide whether they are the same or different. What is one of the ways you know will get you a raise in grades in school?"

B. Student activities
   1. As each item is placed on board, discuss fully and direct students to copy into workbooks.

V. Summary

Teacher says, "For the past two days we have been learning that there are no differences in getting a raise in salary or grades. They are almost exactly the same. Start using these good habits here in school. When you go out on a job you will find these same good habits are the ones you need to be a good worker. What you do in school is the same thing you will do on a job. Learn your good habits here in school and you will have a good attitude for work. Study Days 1, 2 and 3 tonight. Tomorrow we will review the first three days' work and make ourselves a short list of things to do to get a raise in salary or grades."

UNIT VIII   DAYS 2 AND 3

Comparing Raises in Salary with Raises in Grades

(Workbook pages 84–85)

School 1. Do good work.
Work   1. Do good work.
          The same, no different.
School 2. Keep working harder.
Work   2. Keep working harder.
          The same, no different.
School 3. Do neat, clean work.
Work   3. Do neat, clean work.
          The same, no different.

UNIT VIII   DAY 3

(Workbook page 85)

School 4. Keep improving your work.
Work   4. Keep improving your work.
       The same, no different.
School 5. Study your work at night to improve.
Work   5. Study your work at night to improve.
       The same, no different.
School 6. Finish your work completely.
Work   6. Finish your work completely.
       The same, no different.
School 7. Produce more.
Work   7. Produce more.
       The same, no different.
School 8. Be dependable.
Work   8. Be dependable.
       The same, no different.

We can go on forever, and they would be the same. Getting a raise in school grades and a raise in job salary are the same. They are not different.

UNIT VIII   DAY 4

How to Get a Raise in Salary

I. Subject: What to do to get a raise in salary or grades
II. Purpose
   A. To review and reinforce material presented on Days 1, 2 and 3.
   B. To provide a brief listing on "How to Get a Raise."
III. Materials
   A. Teacher materials
     1. Blackboard and chalk

      B. Student materials

          1. Workbook, Unit VIII, Day 4, page 85–86

  IV. Sequence of lesson

      A. Teacher activities

          1. Teacher says, "For the past three lessons we have studied raises in salary and grades. Today I want us to make a short listing of what to do to get a raise in salary and grades. You can use this short listing as a reminder of what to do to raise your grades in school. Let's review what we studied this week and make this listing." (Discuss each item fully.)

      B. Student activities

          1. Have students copy material into their workbooks.

          2. Have students make a large chart listing what to do to get a raise, and display in room.

  V. Summary

Teacher says, "You can use this listing in later life when you are working on a job to remind you how to get a raise. Following this listing will make you a better worker.

"Tomorrow we will study some new words that are important. Some of you may be wondering about the things you should do to get a raise. We have been talking and studying about what to do, but nothing yet about how to do these things. We'll study these later in the unit."

UNIT VIII   DAY 4

What to Do to Get a Raise in Salary or Grades

(Workbook pages 85–86)

  1. What does a raise in salary or grades mean?

     Answer: A raise in salary or grades means getting more money or better grades. Sometimes a raise means getting more happiness on your job.

  2. What can you do to get a raise?

     Answer: A. Do good work.

             B. Work harder

C. Do neat, clean work.

D. Keep improving your work.

E. Study at home.

F. Finish your work completely.

G. Produce more.

H. Be dependable.

3. Is a raise in salary or grades the same?

Answer: A raise in job salary and a raise in grades need the same things. They are no different.

UNIT VIII   DAY 5

How to Get a Raise in Salary

  I. Subject: New vocabulary

 II. Purpose: To introduce new vocabulary used in this unit.

III. Materials

   A. Teacher materials

      1. Blackboard and chalk

   B. Student materials

      1. Workbook, Unit VIII, Day 5, pages 86–87

      2. Dictionary, pencil

IV. Sequence of lesson

   A. Teacher activities

      1. Teacher says, "We are going to learn some new words today. They will be used in this unit and other units which follow. The new words are

1. hour	6. month
2. succeed	7. expect
3. compare	8. cost
4. improve	9. cents
5. produce	

[Drill students on new words.]

    2. "Alphabetize these words and write a simple definition of each word. When you have finished, we'll check your definitions with mine. If yours are very different, change them in your workbook so they will look like mine." (Elicit definitions from students and list on board.)

  B. Student activities

    1. Allow sufficient time for students to alphabetize, find words in their dictionaries, and write definitions in their own words. Nonreaders should be grouped together and given help as needed.

V. Summary

  A. Discuss definitions of words fully. Have students change definitions if they are incorrect. If time allows, review old vocabulary.

  B. Teacher says, "For the next few days we will study how to get a raise in salary or grades. Tonight study Days 1 through 5 in your workbooks."

UNIT VIII   DAY 5

New Vocabulary

(Workbook pages 86–87)

1. Cents: One penny is one cent. 100 cents are one dollar.
2. Compare: To look at two things and see how they are alike or different. When you do this, you compare them.
3. Cost: How much you spend for something. It costs you so much.
4. Expect: When you know something is going to happen, you expect it.
5. Hour: 60 minutes are 1 hour. 24 hours are 1 full day.
6. Improve: To get better. You can improve your work if you try.
7. Month: There are usually 31 days in a month. 12 months are 1 year.
8. Produce: To do something. You produce work on your job.

9. Succeed: To do something well. You hope to succeed on your job.

UNIT VIII   DAYS 6 AND 7

How to Get a Raise in Salary

  I. Subject: How to get that raise
 II. Purpose
    A. To develop in the student the motivation to continue striving harder to improve himself.
    B. To develop in the student a model for learning how to improve himself.
III. Materials
    A. Teacher materials
       1. Blackboard and chalk
    B. Student materials
       1. Workbook, Unit VIII, Days 6 and 7, pages 88–90
 IV. Sequence of lesson
    A. Teacher activities
       1. Teacher says, "Let's review the new words." (Review new words.)
       2. Teacher continues, "We have studied about 'How to Get a Raise in Salary and Grades.' We saw that they were both the same and not different. We learned what to do to get a raise, but we never said anything about how we do these things. Today and tomorrow we're going to study some things that might help us get a raise and see how we can do them. You tell me how you think you can get a raise."
       3. Solicit answers from students to conform to wording shown below. Discuss each listing thoroughly and write on board.
    B. Student activities
       1. Allow students to copy each listing into their workbooks as it is completed on the board.

V. Summary

    A. Teacher says, "Of all the things we listed, which one do you think sort of combines all of the other listings? Yes, number four does. 'Keep Improving and Produce More.' Can you also see how you can do every one of these right here in school? These habits will carry over into anything you will do in your whole lives."

    B. Teacher continues, "Tomorrow we will read a story about Ben and Bob. It has a surprise ending. Bob doesn't get fired. We'll see why tomorrow. Study your workbooks every night. Review past units. You can see how we keep building new information on old units."

UNIT VIII   DAYS 6 AND 7

How to Get That Raise

(Workbook pages 88–90)

Day 6

1. Do good work. How?

    When you start on a job the work is new to you. Your work may not be very good. As you work on the job for a longer time your work will improve. When you start on a job, trying hard to learn will help you do good work. After you have worked awhile, you must do good work or you will be fired from the job. At first you may not even earn your salary.

2. Work harder. How?

    After a time you should be a better worker. When you have learned your job and are earning your salary, don't get lazy. If you only do your job the same way, that's not enough. You must keep working harder. Don't think that just doing your job makes you a better worker. You must keep working harder and produce more. Your boss will fire you if he cannot make any money from your work.

3. Do neat, clean work. How?

    Keep your working place clean. Don't let it get dirty. Keep

the floor clean. Keep your tools put up. Clean your tools every day. Clean other places around the plant. When you finish a job it should be clean and neat. Keep yourself clean and neat. People will respect you for your cleanliness and neatness. Shower every day. Don't be a smelly person. Do not waste material or money.

Day 7

4. Keep improving your work. Produce more. How?

When you start on a job you will be slow. You are still learning. After a month's time you should have learned more about the job. You should be producing more. After a year's time you should have learned still more. You should be producing even faster. If you don't produce more work, you will not get that raise. Your boss pays you for what you produce for the business. Many times a boss will not expect much at first. After a while he will expect more work from you. If you don't improve, he will fire you. He will not keep you if he cannot make any money from your work.

How can you produce more?

Watch the older, better workers. See how they do the work. Try to do it their way. Learn well so you won't waste your time and work. They know a lot of shortcuts to do the job better. Ask them to show you how to use these shortcuts. Your boss will show you how to do the work. Listen carefully and follow directions. Ask smart questions when you are not sure. A good time to ask smart questions is at lunchtime. If you ask when everyone is working, they will waste their time answering your questions. At lunch you are on your own time and not on the boss's time. Try to work faster and better as you learn the job.

5. Study at night. How?

If you can read, go to night school. Take home books from your job. If you cannot read, ask your family to read to you. You can always learn more about your job. The more you learn the better the worker you will be. It will help you produce more.

6. Finish your work completely. How?

Make sure you know what to do. Then do it. Don't leave any

work on your part of the job. A boss likes to see his workers do a finished, neat, clean job. Don't ever have any work left over. Finish it completely.

UNIT VIII   DAY 8

How to Get a Raise in Salary

   I. Subject: A story about Ben and Bob
  II. Purpose
    A. To review the concepts taught in this unit in the form of a short story about two teenagers.
    B. To review Days 1 through 7 via a story.
 III. Materials
    A. Teacher materials: none
    B. Student materials
      1. Workbook, Unit VIII, Day 8, page 91
 IV. Sequence of lesson
    A. Teacher activities
      1. Teacher says, "Today we have a story about Ben and Bob. In this job Bob does not get fired. Maybe he is becoming a better worker. Let's read the story and see what happens."
    B. Student activities
      1. Students read story and discuss it with teacher.
  V. Summary
    A. Teacher should discuss important points with students and answer any questions students pose. Teacher should also use the story to review information from past units.
    B. Teacher says, "Tomorrow, let's examine what's wrong with Bob and what he did wrong and how he could have been a better worker."

Ben and Bob—Surprise! Bob Doesn't Get Fired

If you remember Ben and Bob, you will feel sorry for Ben. Bob was out of a job for about a month, and the family was getting tired of Bob sitting around watching TV and just doing nothing. One of Ben's helpers moved out of town, and Ben's mother asked Ben to try to get Bob the job. Ben didn't want to, but he couldn't say no to his mother. Ben talked to his boss. The boss thought because Bob is Ben's brother, he would be a good worker, too. So Bob went to work at the cafeteria on the dishwashing machine. Well, it didn't take long before everyone found out that Bob was not like his brother Ben. What a difference between them!

Here are some of the stupid things Bob did on the job. He was told never to put dishes and glasses in the machine at the same time. The dishes break the glasses. But he put them in together and broke 14 glasses. The boss made Bob pay for the glasses out of his salary. Bob never finished his work completely. When it was his turn to clean up the dishwashing machine he never finished it. Bob only cleaned what he could see. If he could not see the underneath part of the machine he did not clean it someone always had to do it over again. The other helpers did not like this at all. The cook asked Bob to move a large pot of hot soup. He was told to get someone to help him because the pot was too heavy for one person to carry. But he picked the pot up by himself and dropped it. They were mopping up soup for an hour. Was the boss angry at Bob! He made him pay for the soup out of his salary.

Do you know why Bob was not fired? Well, here is why. His salary at the end of the week came to $12.00. He had worked for 3 days at $4.00 a day. The money to be taken out of his salary was $16.33. If you take the whole $12.00 salary, Bob still owed the boss $4.33. So the boss had Bob come back and work until he could pay the rest of his bill. Then he fired him. Now you know why he didn't get fired!

UNIT VIII   DAY 9

How to Get a Raise in Salary

I. Subject: What's wrong with Bob? How could he improve himself?

II. Purpose: To reinforce and review Unit VIII and material from previous units.

III. Materials

    A. Teacher materials

        1. Blackboard and chalk

    B. Student materials

        1. Workbook, Unit VIII, Days 8 and 9, pages 91–92

IV. Sequence of lesson

    A. Teacher activities

1. Teacher says, "Let's reread yesterday's story and try to list on the board the things that Bob did wrong and how he could improve himself."
2. Read the story, and as wrong actions appear, list them on board (as shown below) and elicit answers from students on how Bob could improve himself.

B. Student activities
1. Students discuss things Bob did wrong and how he could have improved. Teacher writes them on board. Students copy items into workbooks as each item is completed.

V. Summary
Teacher says, "Tomorrow we'll review Unit VIII and have our unit test the next day. Study the entire unit tonight."

UNIT VIII   DAY 9

What's Wrong with Bob? How Could He Improve Himself?

(Workbook pages 91-92)

Wrong   1. Put dishes and glasses in the machine together.
Improve 1. He should have listened to directions and followed them.

Wrong   2. Didn't clean the dishwashing machine well.
Improve 2. He was lazy. He should have listened and followed directions.

Wrong   3. Dropped a pot of soup.
Improve 3. Should have listened to directions and had someone help him.

UNIT VIII   DAY 10

How to Get a Raise in Salary

I. Subject: Review of Unit VIII and Units I, II and III
II. Purpose: To review Units VIII, I, II and III.
III. Materials
   A. Teacher materials: none
   B. Student materials
      1. Workbook, Unit VIII, Days 4, 6, 7, pages 85–86, 88–90; Unit I, Day 11, pages 13–16; Unit II, Day 11, pages 24–26; Unit III, Day 11, pages 35–37.
IV. Sequence of lesson
   A. Teacher activities
      1. Teacher says, "Today we are going to review Unit VIII and Units I, II and III. Tomorrow we will have our test on Unit VIII. There will be questions on the test from units I through III."
      2. Teacher should discuss Days 4, 6 and 7 from Unit VIII. Follow the format shown in teacher activities for each day.
      3. The best technique to review Units I, II and III is to discuss the multiple-choice and the yes-or-no questions from the unit tests. Elicit answers and discussions on the questions and relate the information to Unit VIII and other units.
   B. Student activities
      1. Discussion of material presented by teacher.
V. Summary
Teacher says, "You can see how Unit VIII relates to past units. All the information in each separate unit relates to the others. Tonight study all units carefully and especially Unit VIII. Tomorrow we will have our test on Unit VIII."

UNIT VIII   DAY 11

How to Get a Raise in Salary

I. Subject: Test on Unit VIII
II. Purpose: To test students' grasp of material covered in this unit.
III. Materials
    A. Teacher materials: none
    B. Student materials
        1. Workbook, Unit VIII, Day 11, pages 92–94
        2. Pencil
IV. Sequence of lesson
    A. Teacher activities
        1. Teacher says, "We are having our unit test today. It has three parts. Let's read the directions together." (Read directions to students.)
        2. At conclusion of test, collect workbooks. Grade tests and have workbooks ready to be returned tomorrow for review of test.
    B. Student activities
        1. Students complete test.
V. Summary
Teacher says, "Tomorrow I'll return your tests and we will go over them."

Test on Unit VIII

(Workbook pages 92–94)

Name————————————— Date—————————

Part 1

If you think the sentence is right put a line under Yes. If you think the sentence is wrong put a line under No.

Yes No   1. A raise in salary means that you will get more money.

Yes No   2. You can get a raise without getting more money.

Yes   No   3. Your mother works hard in the home and gets no salary for it.

Yes   No   4. Most times a raise in salary means more money. Sometimes a raise only means more happiness in your job.

Yes   No   5. Getting a raise in job salary is the same as getting a raise in school grades.

Yes   No   6. The habits you use in school to get a raise in grades are the same habits you use to get a raise in job salary.

Yes   No   7. To succeed on a job means that you are doing well.

Yes   No   8. To produce means to do your work well and to do more as you learn more.

Yes   No   9. To improve means that you are not doing very well on your job.

Yes   No   10. As you improve in your work, you will produce more and more.

Part 2

List 8 things you can do in school or on a job to get a raise in grades or salary.
1. Do good work.
2. Work harder.
3. Do neat, clean work.
4. Keep improving.
5. Study at home.
6. Finish your work completely.
7. Produce more.
8. Be dependable.

Part 3

Put these words into the right sentences.
1. cents
2. hour
3. succeed
4. month
5. cost

6. expect
7. produce
8. improve
9. compare
1. 10 cents make a dime.
2. To look at 2 things to see if they are different or alike is to compare.
3. 31 days make 1 month.
4. To do better on a job means you are starting to improve - succeed.
5. 60 minutes make 1 hour.
6. When you know something is coming, you expect it.
7. To turn out more work means you produce more.
8. To pay so much for something is what it costs you.
9. To do well on a job means you succeed on the job.

UNIT VIII   DAY 12

How to Get a Raise in Salary

I. Subject: Review of test on Unit VIII
II. Purpose
   A. To review and reinforce information learned in Unit VIII.
   B. To provide a set of correct answers for student to refer to in later life.
III. Materials
   A. Teacher materials: none
   B. Student materials
      1. Workbook, Unit VIII, Day 11, pages 92–94
      2. Pencil
IV. Sequence of lesson
   A. Teacher activities
      1. Teacher and students should read each question carefully. Teacher should write correct answers on board to serve as a model for students having wrong answers. Allow students sufficient time to change incorrect answers in their workbooks.

   B. Student activities
      1. Students read answers with teacher and correct incorrect answers.
V. Summary
   Teacher says, "Our next unit will be about 'Fifty Ways to Lose Your Job.'"

UNIT IX

Fifty Ways to Lose Your Job

Time required: Twelve days

I. Introduction

A negative approach is usually not the optimum method for teaching positive values. Occasionally, however, this negative technique can be used advantageously to offset a continuous "goody-goody" routine. In this unit there are fifty different suggestions of ways to lose a job. The format for this unit is a simple one. The teacher will ask the students for as many methods as they can think of that could be used to terminate employment. After all the positive values that have been thrown at the students in the past eight units, a simple reversal of these attitudes will indicate various reasons for getting fired. Note that this is a unit that can be used in a shortened space of time preceeding or between the Thanksgiving and/or Christmas holidays. The contents of this unit are actually one concept divided into as many sections as needed. Therefore, all days of instruction are given as one day. There is no test, new vocabulary, or new concept introduced in this unit. The unit should be used as a review, and the teacher should continue the listings into as many days of instruction as desired. Prompt students for listings and enumerate as shown below. Discuss each listing thoroughly with students, especially the how-to-keep-the-job aspects. In order to conserve space in the student workbook, space has been provided for only 10 ways, or three days' work. The unit can readily be continued in the students' notebooks,

and these pages should be added to the workbook as they are
completed.

II. Objectives
   A. Teacher objectives
      1. To develop positive work habits and attitudes via a
         negative approach.
      2. To review contents of all preceding units.
   B. Pupil objectives
      1. To acquire positive attitudes.
      2. To review the concepts of the preceding units.

UNIT IX   DAYS 1 THROUGH 12

Fifty Ways to Lose Your Job

  I. Subject: Fifty ways to lose your job
 II. Purpose
   A. To review Units I through VIII.
   B. To reinforce positive concepts through a negative approach.
III. Materials
   A. Teacher materials
      1. Blackboard and chalk
   B. Student materials
      1. Workbook, Unit IX, pages 94–95
      2. Pen or pencil and notebook
IV. Sequence of lesson
   A. Teacher activities
      1. Teacher says, "This unit is one I think we will have lots
         of fun studying. You will notice that the name of the
         unit is 'Fifty Ways to Lose Your Job.' We are going to
         try in this unit to list fifty ways to lose a job. You will
         tell me what to list, and I will put them on the board.
         Start thinking. Tell me how to lose a job; then we'll list
         under each item how to keep a job. We'll talk about each
         one so we know what was wrong and how to correct it so
         it won't happen to any of us. When we run out of space

in your workbooks we'll continue in your notebooks. Later on, we'll put your notebook pages in your workbooks."

B. Student activities

    1. Students discuss each listing with teacher and copy information into their workbooks or notebooks as it is completed.

V. Summary

    A. The teacher during this listing will find opportune times when it is best to stop and take extra time to discuss a particular item. The entire list of fifty items does not have to be completed in twelve days. Use the listing to reinforce particular items that the students appear interested in. Watch constantly for that "teachable moment." It arises suddenly and at unexpected times. Exploit these moments. Students who are working should be used as reinforcing agents when material is presented.

    B. Teacher says, "Reread these fifty ways and see if you do any of these things here in school or on your job. If you do some of these things, now is the time to change them, while you are still in school. When you leave school or go to work and have these bad habits, they cause you to lose your job. Our next unit is on cooperation. We mentioned this word in one of our earlier units. Next week we'll really study it and see how it will help you succeed here in school and later in life."

UNIT IX DAYS 1–12

Fifty Ways to Lose Your Job

(Workbook pages 94–95)

Day 1

Lose   1. Poor attitude—does not care about his job.
Keep   1. Good attitude—cares for his job.

Lose   2. Careless worker—does things wrong.
Keep   2. Careful worker—does things right.

Lose   3. Only waits for payday—only wants his salary.
Keep   3. Interested in employer's business—wants business to succeed.

Lose   4. Makes same mistakes over and over—poor worker.
Keep   4. Learns each time—watches and listens.

Day 2
Lose   5. Dishonest—steals time and material.
Keep   5. Honest—does not steal. Gives full time to work and never steals.

Lose   6. Has bad manners—acts stupid.
Keep   6. Has nice manners—has a good personality.

Lose   7. Not willing to work—lazy.
Keep   7. Willing to work—good worker and keeps busy.

Lose   8. Lazy—sits around and waits for directions.
Keep   8. Good worker—always busy and keeps working.

Day 3
Lose   9. Does not get along—argues with fellow workers.
Keep   9. Gets along—helps fellow workers, is cooperative.

Lose 10. Will not take orders—does as he pleases.
Keep 10. Will take orders—follows directions.
Continue on in students' notebooks.
Lose 11. Talks back—doesn't like to take orders.
Keep 11. Takes orders—listens and follows instructions.

Lose 12. Absent without good reasons—undependable.
Keep 12. Never absent—dependable.

Day 4
Lose 13. Does not follow directions—does as he pleases.
Keep 13. Follows directions—does what he is told to do.

Lose 14. Undependable—you cannot count on him—unreliable.
Keep 14. Dependable—you can count on him—reliable.

Lose 15. Often late—misses work.
Keep 15. Never late—ready to work on time.

Lose 16. Hasn't learned enough—does not listen.
Keep 16. Has learned enough—listens carefully.

Lose 17. Does not finish job—always has some leftovers.
Keep 17. Finishes job—finishes completely.

Day 5
Lose 18. Does the least he can—lazy.
Keep 18. Does the most he can—hard worker—does extras.

Lose 19. Uncooperative—does not help anyone.
Keep 19. Cooperative—helps everyone.

Lose 20. Starts fights—he makes people fight with him.
Keep 20. Is a good person—people like him. He gets along with everybody.

Lose 21. Is a drinker—drunk sometimes—not safe.
Keep 21. Does not drink—a good safe worker.

Day 6
Lose 22. Dirty, smelly person—does not care for himself.
Keep 22. Clean person—always looks nice and neat.

Lose 23. Won't change wrong ways—won't listen and follow directions.
Keep 23. Will change to right ways—listens and tries to do right thing.

Lose 24. Does not pay his debts—owes everybody.
Keep 24. Does pay his debts—owes nobody—is honest.

Lose 25. A loud, noisy person—nobody respects him.
Keep 25. A nice, quiet person—everybody respects him.

Day 7
Lose 26. Person who picks on people—he ridicules other people.
Keep 26. Person who tends to own business—nice, quiet person.

Lose 27. Poor personality—can't get along with anybody.
Keep 27. Good personality—gets along with everybody.

Lose 28. Quits jobs often—doesn't think much of his job.
Keep 28. Keeps job—respects his job.

Lose 29. Does not try hard—just does not care.
Keep 29. Tries his best—a hard worker.

Day 8
Lose 30. Does not listen or remember—does his work wrong.
Keep 30. Listens and remembers—does his work right.

Lose 31. Wastes time and material—loses money and time for
          his boss.
Keep 31. Never wastes time and material—saves time and money
          for his boss.

Lose 32. Does not like his jobs—quits often.
Keep 32. Likes his job—keeps his jobs.

Lose 33. Rests between work—likes to sit around.
Keep 33. Keeps working—keeps busy.

Day 9
Lose 34. Never looks for work to do—sits around and cheats on
          his time.
Keep 34. Always finds more work—keeps working.

Lose 35. Is a poor student in school—has poor work habits.
Keep 35. Is a good student in school—has good work habits.

Lose 36. Never on time—keeps people waiting for him.
Keep 36. Always on time—keeps his dates on time.

Lose 37. Never ready for work on time—comes late and other
          people have to do his work.
Keep 37. Always ready for work on time—you can count on him.

Day 10
Lose 38. Never works late to finish some work—not reliable.
Keep 38. Always works late when he needs to finish some work—
          very reliable.

Lose 39. Depends on his family to wake him—often late.
Keep 39. Wakes himself—never late.

Lose 40. Often absent, never calls—other workers have to do his
          work.

Keep 40. Only absent for very important reasons—always calls, is reliable.

Lose 41. Lies to people—no one believes him.
Keep 41. Always tells the truth—everyone believes him.

Day 11
Lose 42. Often steals or cheats—not reliable.
Keep 42. Never steals or cheats—very reliable.

Lose 43. Never keeps his word—no one believes him.
Keep 43. Always keeps his word—everybody believes him.

Lose 44. Did not pass a lie-detector test—cheats and steals.
Keep 44. Always passes a lie-detector test—honest.

Lose 45. Cheats on his time during lunch and breaks—dishonest.
Keep 45. Never cheats on his time during lunch and breaks—honest.

Lose 46. Steals tools and material—dishonest.
Keep 46. Never steals anything—honest.

Day 12
Lose 47. Never tries to improve—doesn't care.
Keep 47. Tries to improve—he wants to succeed.

Lose 48. Doesn't produce more—he's a poor worker.
Keep 48. Produces more—he wants that raise in salary.

Lose 49. Doesn't care if he succeeds—will never be a success.
Keep 49. Wants to succeed—he will be a success.

Lose 50. Was not dependable and reliable when he went to school.
Keep 50. Was dependable and reliable when he went to school.

UNIT X

Cooperation Is the Basis of Success

Time required: Twelve days

I. Introduction

This unit is a general overview of methods and techniques of cooperation. An attempt is made in this unit to coordinate the salient facts related to improving one's work situation. The contents are a blend of new and old information. All of the material presented in this unit is pertinent to job success. It offers ten models of personal techniques and five examples of cooperation. The unit tries to inculcate desirable values and concepts into the general background of the retarded person. The extent of the success of this material depends on the attitude of the teacher and whether his method of presentation is enthusiastic.

II. Objectives

A. Teacher objectives

1. To develop in students desirable attitudes of cooperation.
2. To provide examples of cooperation for students to follow.
3. To organize in students a desirable personal model of cooperation.
4. To develop in the group a desirable general knowledge of what cooperation means.

B. Student objectives

1. To acquire desirable attitudes toward cooperation.
2. To acquire a desirable personal model through examples of cooperation.

3. To develop a desirable model of how to cooperate.
4. To acquire a desirable general knowledge of what co-operation means.

UNIT X   DAYS 1 AND 2

Cooperation Is the Basis of Success

I. Subject: Definition of cooperation
II. Purpose
  A. To define cooperation.
  B. To show examples of cooperation.
  C. To develop an awareness of why cooperation is extremely important in the socioeconomic world.
III. Materials
  A. Teacher materials
    1. Blackboard and chalk
  B. Student materials
    1. Workbook, Unit X, Days 1 and 2, pages 96–98
IV. Sequence of lesson
  A. Teacher activities
    1. Teacher says, "This unit is on cooperation. We have used this word before. In this unit we will study cooperation in many different ways. We'll try to give it a good meaning, some examples of cooperation and how to cooperate. Later on in the unit, we'll have some new words, a story, and our usual test at the end of the unit. First, let's find out what cooperation means."
    2. Ask for answers. Prompt and reword students' answers as shown below. Allow students ample time to copy information into their workbooks. This information requires two days to present. On Day 2 merely reintroduce the last information and continue on to that day's work.
  B. Student activities
    1. Students respond with answers which are discussed and placed on board and copied into workbooks.

V. Summary

Teacher says, "For the past two days we have defined cooperation and given some examples of what cooperation is. It is a
word with many answers, all of which make you a better person.
Study these tonight and see if you can pick out the main ideas.
Tomorrow we'll list the main ideas and put them on a large
poster that we may use for review."

UNIT X DAYS 1 AND 2

Some Examples of Cooperation

(Workbook pages 96–98)

1. What does cooperation mean?

   Answer: A. To help other people.

   B. To please other people.

   C. To work well with others.

   D. To do as we are told.

   E. To get along with other people.

2. Can anyone give me some examples of cooperation?

   Answer: Staying late to finish some work. Sometimes our boss
   will ask us to work an extra hour to finish some work
   he needs right away. If we are cooperative, we'll stay
   and gladly do the work. Don't get angry and act bad.
   Smile and say you will be glad to do it. Be sure to call
   home and tell them you will be late. If you don't call,
   your family might wonder why you are late or where
   you are. Your employer will respect you more if you
   do the extra work in a happy way.

3. What is meant by your loyalty to the business?

   Answer: How much you think about the business you work for.
   Are you always talking in a good way about the
   business? Do you tell people what a good place it is
   to work? Do you tell people how good the things
   are that are made there? Are you proud to be working in this business?

Day 2

4. Are you enthusiastic about your work?

    Answer: Are you glad to go to work every day? Do you like your work? A cooperative person is an enthusiastic person. Do you really work hard and do your best? An enthusiastic person is the best worker there is. He is the best.

5. Will you work overtime during busy times of the year?

    Answer: An example of this is that in many businesses things get very busy right before Christmas or other times of the year. Your employer may ask you to work every night for two weeks before Christmas. A cooperative worker will gladly do so. This is the right thing to do. Most of the time you will get extra salary for this overtime work, but not always.

6. Do you like your job?

    Answer: Are you loyal to your job and boss? Some people quit a good job just to make a few dollars a week somewhere else. This is not being loyal. A loyal worker sticks to his job because he likes his job and the people he works with. He cares a lot for it. He is reliable and loyal. A cooperative worker is a loyal worker.

UNIT X   DAY 3

Cooperation Is the Basis of Success

  I. Subject: What a cooperative worker does

 II. Purpose

    A. To review concepts from Days 1 and 2.

    B. To provide a short listing of what a cooperative worker does.

III. Materials

    A. Teacher materials

      1. Blackboard and chalk

      2. Large piece of poster paper and brush pen

   B. Student materials
       1. Workbook, Unit X, Day 3, page 98
       2. Pen or pencil
IV. Sequence of lesson
   A. Teacher activities
       1. Teacher says, "For the past two days we have defined
           cooperation and studied many examples of what a
           cooperative worker does. Today let's see if we can make
           a short listing of what these are so we can have a guide
           to follow. When we're finished, we'll copy these into our
           workbooks and then make a poster. Let's read our work-
           book together aloud and pull out the important ideas
           and list them."
       2. Students and teacher read notes on Days 1 and 2, Unit X,
           and teacher elicits answers as shown in listing below.
           Allow students to copy each listing into their workbooks.
           Have students make large poster with same listing.
   B. Student activities
       1. Students read Unit X, Days 1 and 2 notes in workbook
           and extract pertinent information. These points are dis-
           cussed thoroughly and copied into workbooks.
       2. Have students make large poster with identical listing.
           This should be used to reinforce concepts in review drills.
V. Summary
    Teacher says, "This listing we made today could be an excellent
    way for you to check yourself and see how cooperative you are.
    We'll do this later in the unit. You've noticed that we have been
    using several new words. We'll study the new vocabulary to-
    morrow."

UNIT X   DAY 3

(Workbook page 98)

A cooperative worker will do these things:
1. Help others.
2. Try to please others.
3. Try to work well with others.

4. Get along with almost everyone.
5. Gladly stay late to finish some work.
6. Be loyal to the business.
7. Be enthusiastic about his job and work.
8. Work overtime.

UNIT X   DAY 4

Cooperation Is the Basis of Success

  I. Subject: New vocabulary
 II. Purpose: To introduce new vocabulary used in this unit.
III. Materials
    A. Teacher materials
      1. Blackboard and chalk
    B. Student materials
      1. Workbook, Unit X, Day 4, pages 98–99
      2. Dictionary
      3. Pencil and paper
 IV. Sequence of lesson
    A. Teacher activities
      1. Teacher says, "There are seven new words in this unit. I want you to find them in your dictionary and write a simple definition of each one on some paper. Alphabetize the new words first. When you are finished we'll go over them and put them on the board. Then you'll have a chance to put them in your workbooks."

        1. basis   5. adaptable
        2. example   6. trouble
        3. loyalty   7. interview
        4. enthusiastic

      2. Drill students on words to increase reading knowledge. Allow students to alphabetize words and write own definitions.
      3. Elicit words and definitions from students and place on board. Allow students ample time to correct their answers in workbooks.

B. Student activities
1. Students alphabetize words and look up definitions in dictionary and write own definitions. After teacher and students place correct list on board, students copy correct list of words and definitions into workbooks.

V. Summary

Teacher says, "These words are very important ones. We'll be using them in this and other units. So far we have talked about what to do to be cooperative. During the next few days we'll study about how to be cooperative. The things you actually do to be a cooperative person. Study Days 1, 2, 3 and 4 tonight."

UNIT X   DAY 4

(Workbook pages 98–99)
1. Adaptable: Can be changed easily.
2. Basis: The important part of something. The reason for doing a job is the basis for doing it.
3. Enthusiastic: Being really glad to do something.
4. Example: A good way to do something, that people use to go by when they want to do the same thing.
5. Interview: When you go to see a boss about a job, you have an interview. He interviews you. He looks you over and talks to you.
6. Loyalty: Being true to something. It is important to be loyal to your job.
7. Trouble: A time when things go wrong. Trouble is bad.

UNIT X   DAYS 5 AND 6

Cooperation Is the Basis of Success

I. Subject: How to cooperate
II. Purpose
A. To provide students with models on how to cooperate.
B. To inculcate in students the concept of why we should cooperate.

III. Materials
    A. Teacher materials
        1. Blackboard and chalk
    B. Student materials
        1. Workbook, Unit X, Days 5 and 6, pages 99–102
        2. Pencil
IV. Sequence of lesson
    A. Teacher activities
        1. Teacher says, "For the past few days we have studied some examples of cooperation. We did not say anything about how to act when we cooperate. Today and tomorrow we will talk about how a person can cooperate on a job. There are some things you can do on a job that are good and show that you are cooperative. Can you think of how a good worker can be cooperative?" (Prompt for answers, reword students' answers as shown below. Allow students ample time to copy each answer in workbook as discussion is completed.)
    B. Student activities
        1. Students answer questions and discuss them fully with teacher. After each question students copy answers into their workbooks.
V. Summary
Teacher says, "There are other ways to cooperate. These are only a few of the many ways that you can cooperate. These tell you how to cooperate. You can do these now in school. Learn these good habits now. They are good habits anywhere and especially in later life in anything you do. Tomorrow we will read a story about Ben."

UNIT X   DAYS 5 AND 6

How to Cooperate

(Workbook pages 99–102)
    Day 5
    1. He will work where he is needed.
       He is adaptable to all kinds of work. He will gladly change the

kind of work he is doing if he is needed somewhere else. People who are not cooperative won't change the kind of work they do. A cooperating worker works where he is needed.

2. He is helpful and offers his help.

When work has to be done he does it. He does not wait for a fellow worker or his boss to tell him to help. He knows when there is work to be done, and he does it. He cooperates fully.

3. He takes responsibility.

He is not afraid to do things as long as he is sure what to do. If he is not sure, he leaves the work alone until he can ask good questions on how to do the work. He is able to work by himself. No one has to watch him. He is a responsible, reliable worker. You can leave him alone, and be sure that he is working and not cheating his boss.

4. He tries to save material.

He does not waste any material. If it can be used again he saves it. He knows that this material costs his boss money. He tries to use it well, and not waste it. He's cooperative.

Day 6

5. He doesn't talk back.

He is pleasant and tries to please the people around him. He doesn't look for trouble. He tries to be nice and have a pleasant personality. He's not a troublemaker.

6. He works in a safe manner.

He does not take any chances of getting hurt. He works carefully. If he hurts himself, he cannot work and he loses his salary. He cooperates by working safely.

7. He is ready to try any kind of work if the boss asks him to.

He's not afraid to try something new. As long as his employer asks him to try something new, he will give it a try. He wants good directions to follow from his boss, and he might not do it well at first, but he knows he can learn and can do it better.

8. He tries to improve his work and produce more.

A good worker always tries to improve his work. He never stops trying to improve. This might get him a raise. He tries to produce more so the business he works for will do better.

Ben, the Cooperative Worker Who Succeeded

Ben is a dishwasher in a cafeteria. This is his first job, and he is a little afraid of what is going to happen to him. Anyone going on a new job is a little afraid. He came to work early the first day so his new boss could tell him what to do. He listened carefully to directions, remembered them, and started working. He did not do well at all the first day. He was slow. The other workers had to do some of his work. He forgot a few things, but he asked questions and learned what to do. He kept on trying. The first week he really didn't earn his salary, but his boss saw that he was really trying so he didn't fire him.

It took Ben about two weeks before he really was able to do his share of the work. He tried to please the boss and his fellow workers. He listened and learned. Ben learned slowly, but he tried hard, and his boss liked that. His boss saw that Ben followed directions. After about a month Ben could do his job as well as the other dishwashers. He completely finished any job he started. When his work was finished he did not sit down, but he found work and kept busy. He wasn't the best worker in the cafeteria but he was one of the hardest workers. The boss knew that as long as Ben tried and worked hard he would learn and that soon Ben would be a good worker. Ben was clean and neat in his work. He liked his job and you could see it. He was a quiet, well-mannered person, and people respected him. He took some of the busgirls out on dates and acted like a nice person. He wouldn't bother the girls when they were on the job. After working hours, or at lunchtime, he would talk to them.

Ben succeeded on this job. He is now the head dishwasher, and he has three helpers. He didn't start off very well, but he kept trying and learning. His boss did not mind that he was not a good worker when he started on his job. Ben was a hard worker who kept on trying to improve and produce. The boss could see this right away and didn't fire him.

UNIT X   DAY 7

Cooperation Is the Basis of Success

  I. Subject: Story, "Ben, the Cooperative Worker Who Succeeded"
 II. Purpose
    A. To review Unit X material in story form.
III. Materials
    A. Teacher materials: none
    B. Student materials
      1. Workbook, Unit X, Day 7, page 102
      2. Pencil
IV. Sequence of lesson
    A. Teacher activities
      1. Teacher says, "Let's read this story about 'Ben, the Cooperative Worker Who Succeeded.' As we read it, try to see why Ben did succeed."

B. Student activities
    1. Students and teacher read story.
V. Summary
Teacher says, "This is a true story, and any one of you could or will be Ben someday. That employer knew that as long as Ben tried hard he would succeed. He did succeed. Tomorrow we'll study this story and see what Ben did on his job that made him a success."

UNIT X   DAY 8

Cooperation Is the Basis of Success

  I. Subject: Why did Ben succeed?
 II. Purpose
    A. To reinforce concepts of Unit X in story form.
    B. To provide the basis for a student self-rating scale.
III. Materials
    A. Teacher materials
      1. Blackboard and chalk
    B. Student materials
      1. Workbook, Unit X, Days 7 and 8, page 103
      2. Pencil
IV. Sequence of lesson
    A. Teacher activities
      1. Teacher says, "Today we are going to reread and study the story we read yesterday about Ben. As we read the story let's list on the board why Ben succeeded." (Teacher elicits ideas as shown below, Unit X, Day 8.)
    B. Student activities
      1. Students read story with teacher and select reasons why Ben succeeded. As list is discussed, students copy information into their workbooks.
 V. Summary
Teacher says, "You'll notice that the listing you made in your workbook has a place after it to grade yourself. Tomorrow we'll do this and see how you would do on a job."

UNIT X   DAYS 8 AND 9

(Workbook page 103)

Day 8—Why Ben Succeeded, He   Day 9—Things I Do

	Always 5	Most of the time 4	Some- times 3	Once in a while 2	Never 1
(school)					
1. Came to work early					
2. Listened carefully to directions					
3. Remembered directions					
4. Asked good questions					
5. Learned what to do					
6. Tried hard					
7. Kept on trying					
(students)					
8. Pleased his fellow workers					
(teacher)					
9. Pleased his boss					
10. Listened and learned					
11. Followed directions					
12. Completely finished his job					
13. Found extra work, kept busy					
14. Was clean and neat					
15. Was enthusiastic					
16. Had quiet, good manners					
17. Was respected by other people					
18. Was honest in his work					
19. Improved and produced more					
20. Was responsible and dependable					
My score					

UNIT X   DAY 9

Cooperation Is the Basis of Success

I. Subject: Student self-rating scale on cooperation
II. Purpose: To review Unit X and contents of other units via a student self-rating scale.
III. Materials
   A. Teacher materials
      1. Blackboard and chalk
   B. Student materials
      1. Workbook, Unit X, Day 8, page 103
      2. Pencil
IV. Sequence of lesson
   A. Teacher activities
      1. Teacher says, "Yesterday we made a list of why Ben succeeded on his job. To prove that work and school are the same we'll take the same fact list and rate ourselves." (Explain rating system to students as in previous units. Read each item with students as they rate themselves.) "All we have to do is change the word school to work in Number 1, workers to students in Number 8, and boss to teacher in Number 9."
      2. Allow students to rate themselves. Have them add scores and divide by 20. Determine the class average and explain their scores to them. Impress on students that any of the 20 items that had a score of three or below is a failing grade on a job and that they should pay special attention to these columns.
   B. Student activities
      1. Students rate themselves and compare their scores to class average.
V. Summary
Teacher says, "Anyone who made a score of three or below on any item would have a hard time keeping his job. Try very hard to improve any items you made a three or less on. Let's

talk about these items and see if and how we can raise them.
Tomorrow we'll review Units IV, V and VI. Read them tonight.
Ask your family to read them to you if you have trouble reading
them yourself."

UNIT X   DAY 10

Cooperation Is the Basis of Success

   I. Subject: Review of Units X, IV, V and VI
  II. Purpose: To review information in Units X, IV, V and VI.
 III. Materials
    A. Teacher materials
      1. Unit X, Days 1, 2, 5 and 6; Unit IV, Day 11, Part 1;
      Unit V, Day 11, Part 1; Unit VI, Day 11, Part 2
    B. Student materials
      1. Same as teacher materials
  IV. Sequence of lesson
    A. Teacher activities
      1. Teacher should review days listed above in teacher
      materials. Discuss items which appear to be more mean-
      ingful to students. Use working students' remarks to
      reinforce teacher comments. In Units IV, V and VI, read
      questions with students and discuss fully.
    B. Student activities
      1. Students discuss material with teacher.
   V. Summary
Teacher says, "Tomorrow we will have our test on Unit X.
Study the entire unit tonight."

UNIT X   DAY 11

Cooperation Is the Basis of Success

   I. Subject: Test on Unit X
  II. Purpose: To test students' knowledge of material covered in this
unit.

III. Materials
   A. Teacher materials: none
   B. Student materials
      1. Workbook, Unit X, Day 11, pages 104–106
IV. Sequence of lesson
   A. Teacher activities
      1. Teacher says, "We are having our unit test today. There are four parts to the test. Let's read the directions together. [Read directions for each part.] Begin."
      2. The teacher can test the nonreaders' knowledge by administering the test verbally. If there is insufficient time, have one of the better reading students, after he has finished the test, read the questions to a nonreading student. Teacher should collect workbooks and grade test. Return workbooks next day for discussion of test.
   B. Student activities
      1. Students take test.
 V. Summary
   Teacher says, "I will collect your workbooks, grade your tests, and return them tomorrow. Tomorrow we will go over the test and you will have the opportunity to see what questions you had wrong and to correct them."

Test on Unit X

(Workbook pages 104–106)

Name_____ Date_____

Part 1

Give 5 examples of what a good worker can do for the business he works for to be cooperative.
1. Staying late to finish some work.
2. Loyalty to business.
3. Enthusiastic about his job.
4. Work overtime if he has to.
5. Likes his job.

Part 2

Name 8 things to show how a good worker acts in his work to be cooperative.
1. Helps others.
2. Tries to please others.
3. Tries to work well with others.
4. Gets along with almost everyone.
5. Gladly stays late to finish his work if asked to.
6. Is loyal to the business.
7. Is enthusiastic about his job and work.
8. Will work overtime.

Part 3

Put a line under the word Yes if you think the sentence is right. Put a line under the word No if you think the sentence is wrong.

Yes No 1. Cooperation means to have a poor attitude.
Yes No 2. If your boss asks you to work a little later to finish some work, tell him no.
Yes No 3. Always say bad things about the business or place you work.
Yes No 4. When you are not enthusiastic about your job, you are usually a cooperative worker.
Yes No 5. When business is busy, do not work overtime.
Yes No 6. When you like your job and work hard, you can succeed at it.
Yes No 7. A lazy worker is a good example to follow.
Yes No 8. An adaptable worker will change work places and work where he is needed.
Yes No 9. When you keep doing your work wrong and do not learn the right way, you are in trouble.
Yes No 10. A cooperative worker helps where he is needed. He does not have to be asked. He offers his help.

Part 4

Extra credit: You cannot lose. If your answers are wrong, no points are taken off. If your answers are right, you can earn extra points on your grade.

Give the meanings of these 15 words in your own words.

1. interview	9. reliable
2. important	10. truth
3. ridicule	11. steal
4. business	12. improve
5. directions	13. debts
6. personality	14. trouble
7. habits	15. produce
8. understand	

UNIT X   DAY 12

Cooperation Is the Basis of Success

I. Subject: Review of Unit X
II. Purpose
   A. To review contents of Unit X by going over test on Unit X.
   B. To provide a set of correct answers for students to refer to in later life.
III. Materials
   A. Teacher materials
      1. Blackboard and chalk
   B. Student materials
      1. Workbook, Unit X, Day 11, pages 104–106
      2. Pencil
IV. Sequence of lesson
   A. Teacher activities
      1. Teacher should review all questions on Unit X test. Emphasize and discuss more fully the portions of the test on which students had difficulty. Write correct answers on the board to parts 1, 2 and 4, so students can copy correct answers.
   B. Student activities
      1. Students review the test with teacher and discuss fully any portion of the test with which they had difficulty.
      2. Students correct answers in their workbooks.

V. Summary
Teacher says, "I hope you were able to understand the different definitions of cooperation and how important they are to your success in holding a job. Our next unit will be on your attitude and its importance to your success or failure."

UNIT XI

Your Attitude Means Success or Failure

Time required: Twelve days

I. Introduction

Certain basic attitudes and values which contribute to adult success have been presented in the preceding ten units. To help insure changes in student behavior, there has been a constant repetition of important information. This unit continues to follow the format of presenting new material and reviewing old material. Basically, this unit is the crux of all the aims and objectives of these occupational education units. The next, and concluding, unit is concerned with going for a job interview, and attempts to traverse from job preparation to job-holding. This unit attempts to summarize all materials presented previously and unify them into criteria exemplifying a successful person. If this concept of a successful person can be acquired by these retarded students, it can serve as a model for adulthood.

II. Objectives

A. Teacher objectives

1. To develop a desirable definition of what is considered success in adulthood.

2. To provide a checklist of accepted, successful work habits.

B. Student objectives
  1. To acquire a desirable concept and model for successful adulthood.
  2. To acquire a checklist of desirable work habits that can be used through adulthood.

UNIT XI   DAYS 1, 2, 3 AND 4

Your Attitude Means Success or Failure

  I. Subject: The difference between a successful and an unsuccessful person
 II. Purpose
  A. To teach the concept of how a successful person interacts with society.
  B. To teach the concept of how an unsuccessful person interacts with society.
  C. To develop a model of a successful person.
III. Materials
  A. Teacher materials
    1. Blackboard and chalk
  B. Student materials
    1. Workbook, Unit XI, Days 1, 2, 3 and 4, pages 106–110
    2. Pencil
 IV. Sequence of lesson
  A. Teacher activities
    1. This unit entails four days of presentation. Follow the format shown for Day 1 on subsequent days. Discuss fully each topic. Working students can serve as reinforcing agents.
    2. Teacher says, "In this school year we have been studying the different ways to be a successful worker. We have tried to tell you how to become a good worker. We have not said very much about the rest of your lives. Working and holding a job are only part of your lives. If you are a successful worker, will this affect the rest of your life?

What becomes of you if you are successful or unsuccessful? What kind of life do you want to live? How will you live if you are successful, and how will you live if you are a failure?

"For the next few days I want you to give me some examples of how a successful person lives and then we will compare them to how an unsuccessful person lives. Then you can decide which kind of life you want to live. Think of the successful people you know. How do they live? What do they do that shows they are successful? Think of answers to this question: How does a successful person live as compared to an unsuccessful person?"

B. Student activities

    1. Students copy information from board into their workbooks as each item is completed.

V. Summary

Teacher says, "Look at this list. Which kind of person are you now? Which kind of person will you be? You know what to do and how to do things right. But no one can decide for you. You must decide for yourself. Keep this workbook for the rest of your life. It can help tell you the difference between a successful and an unsuccessful person. After you finish school and go to work, there will be many times when you are not sure of how to act, so read this workbook over so you will remember. Do not ever forget what is in this workbook. It may change your whole life. It could mean the difference between being a successful person or an unsuccessful person. Tomorrow we'll study a few new words that are important for you to know."

UNIT XI   DAYS 1, 2, 3 AND 4

The Difference Between a Successful and an Unsuccessful Person

(Workbook pages 106–110)

Day 1
Successful   1. Keeps his job—does not quit or get fired.
Unsuccessful 1. Loses his jobs—quits or gets fired.

Successful   2. Brings home a salary every payday.
Unsuccessful   2. Has no salary or money he has earned.

Successful   3. Has his own money for the things he needs.
Unsuccessful   3. Has to wait for his family to give him money. He is always poor.

Successful   4. Gives his family money for his room and board.
Unsuccessful   4. Does not give his family any money for anything. He takes.

Successful   5. Has enough of his own spending money for the things he needs.
Unsuccessful   5. Asks his family to give him spending money.

Day 2
Successful   6. Buys his own clothes when he needs them.
Unsuccessful   6. Waits for his family to buy him some clothes.

Successful   7. Saves some money every payday for the day when he may need extra money.
Unsuccessful   7. Cannot save any money at all.

Successful   8. Gets along with people.
Unsuccessful   8. Does not get along with people.

Successful   9. Goes to work every day. Is reliable and enthusiastic.
Unsuccessful   9. Sits at home and does nothing.

Successful   10. He is producing things for other people on his job.
Unsuccessful   10. He only takes. He produces nothing.

Day 3
Successful   11. Is with other people every day.
Unsuccessful   11. Sits at home alone.

Successful   12. Gets out into the world around him. He is adaptable.
Unsuccessful   12. He just sits at home. He is partly dead in his mind.

Successful 13. He has dates with other people. He has money and friends.

Unsuccessful 13. He sits at home alone. He has no money or friends.

Successful 14. He studies and tries to improve himself.

Unsuccessful 14. He has nothing to study and will not improve himself.

Successful 15. He goes to church and belongs to the young people's group.

Unsuccessful 15. He stays home or stands around on street corners.

Successful 16. He is respected because he gives of himself to the people around him.

Unsuccessful 16. He is ridiculed because he only takes from the people around him.

Day 4

Successful 17. He wants to get married someday and have his own home.

Unsuccessful 17. He cannot marry because he cannot earn any money.

Successful 18. He is a happy, pleasant person.

Unsuccessful 18. He is almost always a sad person.

Successful 19. You are proud to have him as your friend.

Unsuccessful 19. You do not care if he is your friend.

Successful 20. He is an honest, good person and has no troubles.

Unsuccessful 20. He is not always honest and sometimes gets into trouble with the police.

Successful 21. He pays his debts. His word is the best.

Unsuccessful 21. He owes everybody. No one believes him.

UNIT XI   DAY 5

Your Attitude Means Success or Failure

  I. Subject: New vocabulary
 II. Purpose: To introduce the new vocabulary used in this unit.
III. Materials
    A. Teacher materials
      1. Blackboard and chalk
    B. Student materials
      1. Workbook, Unit XI, Day 5, pages 110–111
      2. Dictionary
      3. Pencil and paper
IV. Sequence of lesson
    A. Teacher activities
      1. Teacher says, "We have eight new words in this unit. On a sheet of paper I want you to alphabetize them and then find them in your dictionary. Write a simple meaning for each word. We'll check them on the board and then you can copy them in your workbook."
      The new words are:

      1. fail   3. group 5. rate   7. responsibility
      2. church 4. marry 6. decision 8. minister

      (Drill students on reading knowledge and comprehension.)
      2. Allow ample time for students to find words and write definitions. List words on board as shown and elicit answers from students. Allow ample time to copy information into workbooks.
    B. Student activities
      1. Students find answers in dictionary and write definitions in own words, then copy material from blackboard into their workbooks.
 V. Summary
    Teacher says, "If your words and definitions are not the same as

those on the board, then change them so they are the same. Learn these words well. Tomorrow we are going to rate ourselves on our attitudes. You will see some of these words on the rating sheet. Know them."

UNIT XI   DAY 5

(Workbook pages 110–111)

1. Church: A place we go to pray to God on Sunday.
2. Decision: When we have to think about something and know what to do, we have to make a decision. We must decide what to do.
3. Fail: Not to pass is to fail. If we do not do something right, we fail to do it.
4. Group: When several people get together they are a group.
5. { Marriage / Marry } : When two people fall in love and want to live together for the rest of their lives, they get married. You must think marriage over very carefully and ask your families what they think about it.
6. Minister: The man who leads you in prayer in church. He is a good friend to have. He can help you answer a lot of your questions.
7. Rate: To rate yourself is to give yourself a grade on something you do.
8. Responsibility: When you do things on your own, when you make a decision of your own, you are showing responsibility.

UNIT XI   DAY 6

Your Attitude Means Success or Failure

I. Subject: Rate yourself
II. Purpose
  A. To review important material presented in first ten units.

  B. To reinforce old material in the form of a self-rating check-list applicable to school or work.

  C. To have students rate themselves on this checklist.

III. Materials

  A. Teacher materials: none

  B. Student materials

   1. Workbook, Unit XI, Day 6, pages 111–113

   2. Pen or pencil

IV. Sequence of lesson

  A. Teacher activities

   1. Teacher says, "Today we are going to rate ourselves. Turn to page 112 in your workbook and you will find 33 sentences on which you will give yourself a grade of Always, Most of the Time, Sometimes, Once in a While, or Never. If you have learned the material well in these units and changed your personality for the better, you should make a good grade. If you make a high grade, then you have a good attitude and personality. If you do these things every day you are ready for a job, and you should succeed. Remember, you must keep on doing these things forever. Not only today, or this week, or month, but for the rest of your lives. Open your work-books to Unit XI, page 111. Listen to the directions before you start." (Teacher then reads directions to students, workbook, page 111.)

  B. Student activities

   1. Students rate themselves and grade rating scales with teacher.

   2. Teacher says, "Here is how to grade yourself. For every Always, give yourself 5 points. For every Most of the Time, give yourself 4 points. For every Sometimes, give yourself 3 points. For every Once in a While, give your-self 2 points and for every Never, 1 point."

V. Summary

Teacher says, "If your grade is 165, that is the best you or any-one else can do. A grade of less than 165 means that you have to improve until you can answer Always to every question. Keep on trying; you can do it. Use this test as a way to improve yourself. See what things need improving. Work on these every day here in school or in your job. Learn these good habits so you can be a success in life. Study these ratings. Do not ever lose them. They can help you for the rest of your life. Tomorrow we have a story about how Ben meets Ginger."

UNIT XI DAY 7

Your Attitude Means Success or Failure

I. Subject: The Story "Ben Meets Ginger"
II. Purpose: To reinforce new and old material in the form of a story.
III. Materials
   A. Teacher materials: none
   B. Student materials
      1. Workbook, Unit XI, Day 7, page 114
IV. Sequence of lesson
   A. Teacher activities
      1. Teacher says, "We are going to review the material we learned in this unit. We have a story called 'Ben Meets Ginger.' Remember them? They were the successful people. Bob and Jane never did succeed. They are not working now. They are sitting home, taking from their families."
   B. Student activities
      1. Students read story with teacher and discuss each important idea fully.
V. Summary
   Teacher says, "This story could be about any one of you. Wait for the right time, be successful, save your money and you will meet that certain boy or girl. When you do, be wise, think it over, and when things are right you may get married also. But all this takes time and money. It is always better to wait and talk it over with your families. Tomorrow I want to go over the story and see if we can find the things that made Ben and Ginger successful."

How Do You Rate? Do You Have a Good Attitude?

How to rate yourself: Put a check under *Always* if you do it always every day. Put a check under *Most of the Time* if you do not do it most of the time. Put a check under *Sometimes* if you are trying to do this, and do it sometimes. Put a check under *Once in a While* if you are trying to improve. Put a check under *Never* if you never do this. Put only 1 answer to each question. Be honest and truthful in your answers. You cannot fool yourself.

Things I Do:	Always 5	Most of the time 4	Sometimes 3	Once in a while 2	Never 1
1. Get along with other students or workers					
2. Have nice manners and know how to meet people					
3. Know how to make a decision by myself					
4. Am willing to take directions, with no talking back					
5. Am willing to do same job over and over again					
6. Am willing to take on some responsibility					
7. Am always neat and clean					
8. Am a steady, reliable worker					
9. Do not get angry when I am told that I am wrong and am told how to do it right					
10. Want to work					
11. Want an honest salary or grade and do not ask for too much salary or too high a grade					
12. Am on time every day					
13. Want to please people around me					
14. Keep my work place clean and neat					
15. Am reliable and on the job every day					
16. Am honest all the time					
17. Do not easily get angry					
18. Am a nice quiet person					

Things I Do:	Always 5	Most of the time 4	Sometimes 3	Once in a while 2	Never 1
19. Am loyal to my job or school					
20. Work safely and carefully					
21. Keep trying even if I am slow and do not do very good work at first					
22. Take good care of myself and do not get sick					
23. Am a cooperative person					
24. Work on my own and do not always have to be told what to do					
25. Never cheat on my work or time					
26. Keep on working harder and producing more for that raise in grade or salary					
27. Finish my work completely					
28. Do not waste time or material					
29. Do the extras without being asked					
30. Know how to stay away or get away from a person who ridicules me					
31. Want to succeed and will work hard so that I can succeed					
32. Am the kind of person you would want for a friend					
33. Am the kind of person you want working with you					
MY SCORE:					

Ben Meets Ginger

Ben is such a nice person, and Ginger is such a nice girl, why shouldn't they meet? Here is how it happened. Ginger went to church and belonged to the young people's group. They met two times a week for church meetings. They played games, danced, or just talked. They went on picnics, to the movies, and other places together. They had good times. All of them worked and earned the money to spend for these good times. Most of them were about 18 to 21 years old. Some of them were going steady and were going to get married. It was a fine group. None of them hung around street corners, or got into any trouble. You would be proud to be in this group.

Ben went to the same church but was afraid to join this young people's group. One day the minister of the church asked Ben to join. Ben just said no because he had no way to get to church for the meetings. The minister was smart. He told Ben that he would pick him up and bring him. Ben couldn't get out of that. He came to the meeting with the minister. Yes, you are right. He met Ginger. They liked each other right away. That minister was a real friend to make Ben join the group.

Ben and Ginger liked a lot of the same things. They were both successful. They had good jobs, and saved some of their salary every payday. Ben had enough money to take Ginger out for dates. When he was getting low on money, Ginger would invite Ben to her home. Soon they were going steady. Ben bought Ginger a ring. Ben paid for it. He had saved up the money and had it when he needed it. They want to get married soon. They know that they will need lots more money before they can marry. Ben and Ginger are both saving toward that day. They want to be able to pay for their household goods. They do not want to go into debt. They will make it. It may take a while, but they will use their heads and get married when they feel that they can. It's wonderful to be successful and meet the right boy or girl. You might too, someday.

UNIT XI DAY 8

Your Attitude Means Success or Failure

I. Subject: Why were Ben and Ginger successful?
II. Purpose: To reinforce and review Unit XI in story form.
III. Materials
  A. Teacher materials
    1. Blackboard and chalk
    2. Brush pen and poster paper
  B. Student materials
    1. Workbook, Days 7 and 8, pages 114–115
    2. Pen or pencil
IV. Sequence of lesson
  A. Teacher activities

      1. Teacher and students read story, Unit XI, Day 7. As story is read, teacher elicits important ideas from class to correspond with listing shown below, Unit XI, Day 8.

  B. Student activities

      1. Students read story, Unit XI, Day 7, with teacher.

      2. Students and teacher select important concepts from story and teacher places them on board.

      3. Students copy concepts into workbooks.

      4. Students ink poster with concepts listed.

V. Summary

Teacher says, "For the past two days we have studied why Ben and Ginger were successful people. Tomorrow we'll read a story about Bob and what he is doing now."

UNIT XI   DAY 8

How to Be a Successful Person

(Workbook pages 114–115)

1. Be a nice person.
2. Work and earn money.
3. Have a good job.
4. Save some money.
5. Do not go into debt.
6. Pay as you buy.
7. Join a church.

UNIT XI   DAY 9

Your Attitude Means Success or Failure

I. Subject: The story "What Happened to Bob?"

II. Purpose: To reinforce a model of a successful adult via a story of an unsuccessful person.

III. Materials

 A. Teacher materials: none

 B. Student materials

  1. Workbook, Unit XI, Day 9, page 115

IV. Sequence of lesson

 A. Teacher activities

  1. Teacher reads story about Bob. Discuss fully the under-lined phrases, comparing Bob's behavior with that of a successful person.

  2. Teacher says, "Today we're going to read a story about Bob. If you remember, he's Ben's brother and was always getting fired from his job. Let's see how he's doing now."

 B. Student activities

  1. Students read story and discuss story with teacher.

V. Summary

Teacher says, "Well, which person do you want to be, Ben or Bob? The only person who can decide is yourself. Tomorrow we'll review this unit and other units and get ready for our unit test."

What Happened to Bob?

Bob is now staying at home. He sort of stopped looking for a job. He was fired from so many jobs that he gave up trying to earn his own living. He just doesn't do much. He gets up late every morning, usually about 10 or 11. Everyone in the family works, so he's home alone all day. He eats breakfast. He never cooks anything. He just eats some cake and milk. His face is beginning to show it. Then he sits around in his underwear and watches TV and eats candy or peanuts if there are any around. Yes, he's getting fat. His clothes are too tight, but he can't buy any new clothes because he has no money. His family won't give him any money. They feel that a grown man should be working and buying his own things. In the afternoon he sleeps and when he wakes up he takes a walk. He has no friends his age because people his age are working. He hangs around the street corner with some high school kids after they get out of school. He's about three or four years older than they are. These boys have no respect for him because he never works and never has any money.

He got into trouble with the police one time because he stole something out of an open parked car. This scared him, so he never tried to steal again. Sometimes when he needs money he would like to steal but he's afraid to. He doesn't ever want to fool with those police again. When he wants some money, he begs for it from his family. It's sort of sad to see a grown man beg for money. No one has any respect for him. Would you? He's thought of going to work but he just can't get himself to really look for a job. He doesn't seem to respect himself at all.

His family have given up on him. They think he'll never be anything. He never did learn good habits or how to hold a job. Bob is a good person but he never did learn to be dependable and reliable. What a waste of a good person!

UNIT XI   DAY 10

Your Attitude Means Success or Failure

   I. Subject: Review of Units XI, VII, VIII and IX
  II. Purpose
    A. To review Unit XI and past units.
    B. To prepare students for test on Unit XI.
 III. Materials
    A. Teacher materials: none
    B. Student materials
       1. Workbook, Unit XI, Days 1, 2, 3 and 4; Units VII, VIII and IX, Days 11
  IV. Sequence of lesson
    A. Teacher activities
       1. Teacher should review Days 1, 2, 3 and 4. Discuss briefly all items. Discuss fully any items students have more difficulty comprehending.
       2. Review unit tests for Units VII, VIII and IX. Usually unit tests are the best form of review. Select portions of tests that have most meaning to students.
    B. Student activities
       1. Students discuss items with teacher.
   V. Summary
Teacher says, "Tonight I want you to study all of Unit XI. Read your workbooks over completely. Tomorrow we'll have our test on Unit XI."

UNIT XI   DAY 11

Your Attitude Means Success or Failure

   I. Subject: Test on Unit XI
  II. Purpose: To determine students' grasp of material covered in this unit.

III. Materials
    A. Teacher materials: none
    B. Student materials
        1. Workbook, Unit XI, Day 11, pages 116–118
        2. Pen or pencil
IV. Sequence of lesson
    A. Teacher activities
        1. Teacher says, "We are having our unit test today. I hope that you have all studied and will make a good grade on it. Let's read the directions together." (Read directions shown on test for each part. Collect workbooks, grade and return the following school day.)
    B. Student activities
        1. Students take test.
  V. Summary
Teacher says, "I will grade these tonight and return them tomorrow. We'll go over them and you will be able to correct your mistakes."

Test on Unit XI

(Workbook pages 116–118)

Name_____ Date_____

Part 1

Here are 20 sentences about a successful or unsuccessful person. If you think the sentence means they are successful, put a line under Yes. If you think the sentence means that they are not successful, put a line under the word No.

Yes (No   1. Loses his job often.
(Yes) No   2. Brings home his salary every payday.
Yes No   3. Asks his family for spending money.
Yes No   4. Pays for his room and board.
Yes No   5. Has earned his own spending money.
Yes No   6. Buys his own clothes when he needs them.

Yes No   7. Does not save any money.
Yes No   8. Gets along with people.
Yes No   9. Is reliable.
Yes No 10. Is not dependable.
Yes No 11. Likes to be with people.
Yes No 12. Sits at home alone.
Yes No 13. Pays his debts.
Yes No 14. You can't depend on his word.
Yes No 15. Tries hard to improve and produce more.
Yes No 16. Is ridiculed often.
Yes No 17. Is a respected person.
Yes No 18. Gets into lots of trouble.
Yes No 19. Is always on time.
Yes No 20. Is a good, honest person.

Part 2

Each sentence has at least one right answer. If there is more than one right answer, underline all the right answers. Look over the answers carefully so you won't miss any right answers.

1. A responsible person will
    A. Cheat on his time.
    B. Waste material.
    C. Work on his own.
2. When you make a decision you must
    A. Think over what to do.
    B. Make sure you know what is best to do.
    C. Know the right thing to do, be sure, then do it.
3. A minister works in a
    A. Cleaning plant.
    B. School.
    C. Church.
4. When we fail in our work we
    A. Get a raise in salary.
    B. Get fired from our job.
    C. Make a failing grade.
5. Ginger and Bob were
    A. Successful people.

   B. Wise people.
   C. Dumbbells.
6. If you make a grade of 165 on the rating sheet, you can
   A. Stop trying.
   B. Keep on trying.
   C. Not care.
7. When you must be told what to do over and over, you are
   A. Responsible.
   B. Reliable.
   C. Not dependable.
8. Why will you be successful? Because you
   A. Listened and studied these units.
   B. Learned good habits in school.
   C. Took these good habits to the job.
9. A successful person will
   A. Save all his money.
   B. Spend all of his money.
   C. Spend part and save part of his money.
10. Would you like to be like
    A. Ginger and Ben?
    B. Jane and Bob?
    C. All four of them?

Part 3

This is an extra credit question. You cannot lose any points. Get it right for extra points.
1. List 10 things that show you are a successful person.
   (Any 10 items describing a successful person.)

UNIT XI   DAY 12

Your Attitude Means Success or Failure

  I. Subject: Review of test on Unit XI
 II. Purpose
     A. To review and reinforce contents of Unit XI.

B. To provide a set of correct answers in students' workbooks for them to follow in later life.

III. Materials
  A. Teacher materials: none
  B. Student materials
    1. Workbook, Unit XI, Day 11, pages 116–118

IV. Sequence of lesson
  A. Teacher activities
    1. Teacher should go over all questions, allowing students time to correct wrong answers. Discuss fully any portions of test students had difficulty with. This review is an excellent teaching device and should be used to the fullest.
  B. Student activities
    1. Students go over test and correct wrong answers.

V. Summary
Teacher says, "Your answers should all be correct. When you finish school and go to work, this workbook should be a guide to you. It tells you how to act as a person working on a job. You can always reread it to remind you of the right things to do. Our next unit is on how to go for a job interview."

UNIT XII

Going for Your First Job Interview

Time required: Twelve days

I. Introduction

Unit XII is the final one in this series. The objective of this unit is to transfer the student from the school phase of job preparation to his first job interview. Preparing and going for a job interview in itself could easily be divided into many units of instruction. Because of the time factor, however, only one unit is being presented. Again the teacher should stress the fact that good habits are developed in school and carried over into the socioeconomic world. The entire set of units has as its primary aim the concept that the material presented will be of value to secondary school mentally retarded students in the adult world. Much of the value of the units depends on the enthusiasm of the teacher, and the way they are implemented by the students in their school environment.

II. Objectives

   A. Teacher objectives

      1. To develop realistic attitudes toward a job interview.

      2. To develop some concept of what to expect in a job interview.

      3. To develop the correct model of physical appearance for the job interview.

      4. To develop a correct model of mental attitude for the job interview.

        5. To review the basic concepts presented in the complete
set of units.
- B. Pupil objectives
  1. To acquire a desirable attitude toward the job interview.
  2. To develop the concept of what to expect in a job interview.
  3. To prepare his physical appearance for the job interview.
  4. To acquire a role of mental alertness for the job interview.
  5. To review and synthesize the information presented in all units.

UNIT XII   DAYS 1 AND 2

Going for Your First Job Interview

  I. Subject: Getting ready for a job interview
 II. Purpose
- A. To define a job interview.
- B. To develop a model of how to prepare oneself mentally and physically for a job interview.

III. Materials
- A. Teacher materials
  1. Blackboard and chalk
- B. Student materials
  1. Pencil
  2. Workbook, Unit XII, Days 1 and 2, pages 118–120

IV. Sequence of lesson
- A. Teacher activities
  1. The information entails two days of presentation. Day 2 follows Day 1 without any interruption in material.
  2. Teacher says, "Many of you will be finishing school this year, or in another year or two. Whether you finish school or not, you will have to go and look for a job. Finishing school will be a big help to you. Most employers will not hire anyone who has not finished high school. Most of you will be afraid to go for your first job

interview. Most people are afraid the first time they go looking for a job. This is understandable. Don't feel bad about being afraid.

"In this unit we are going to study about the job interview. We will study the job interview in three parts. First, we'll talk about getting ready. Then, we'll discuss how to behave. Last, we'll talk about the kind of questions you will have to answer. Later on in this unit we have a story about Ginger looking for a job.

"Let's begin with today's work. I'm going to ask you some questions. You start thinking and give me the answers. I'll put them on the board." (Reword answers as shown below.)

B. Student activities
1. Students answer questions and discuss them fully. As each section is completed on the board, students transfer it into their workbooks.

V. Summary
Teacher says, "We have talked about how to get ready for a job interview. Tomorrow we'll put these into a short listing and put this listing in your workbooks and on a poster. Tonight I want you to think about these points and write down what you think would be a good, short guide to anyone going for a job interview."

UNIT XII   DAYS 1 AND 2

Getting Ready for Your First Job Interview

(Workbook pages 118–120)

Day 1

What can you do to get ready for your first job interview? There are many things you can do. Let's list them.

1. Decide what kinds of work you want to do. Do not decide on only one kind of work. Pick several kinds of work that you think you can and will be able to do. Be especially careful of jobs that need lots of reading. Go to businesses that have the

kinds of work you think you can do. You don't always get the first job you look for. There are many kinds of jobs to look for.

2. You are supposed to be a little scared. Most people are. It's all right to be scared. Try not be so scared that you shake or cannot talk. It is better to be scared a little, but not too much.

3. Go alone. Do not take anyone with you. Show your boss that you can come by yourself. It helps to show that you are a responsible person.

4. Be on time. Allow plenty of time to get there. Come early.

Day 2

5. Look your best. How?

   A. Shower and get clean.

   B. Boys: Dress in a white shirt and tie. Wear dress pants and a coat. Be sure all the colors go together. If you are not sure, ask your family to help you pick your clothes and colors. If you have a Sunday suit, wear it. Look as nice as when you are going to church on Sunday.

   C. Girls: Do not use too much make-up. Just a little bit will be better. Wear a nice dark dress. A dress you would wear to church is fine. Wear stockings and make sure they stay up. If you are not sure what to wear, ask your family. You will be all right if you wear clothes you wear to church on Sunday.

UNIT XII   DAY 3

Going for Your First Job Interview

  I. Subject: Short listing of how to get ready for a job interview

 II. Purpose

   A. To review concepts presented in Days 1 and 2.

   B. To provide a short listing of steps in getting ready for a job interview to serve as a guide in future life.

III. Materials

   A. Teacher materials

     1. Blackboard and chalk

     2. Poster paper and brush pen

B. Student materials
1. Workbook, Unit XII, Day 3, page 120
2. Pencil
IV. Sequence of lesson
A. Teacher activities
1. Teacher says, "For the past two days we have talked about getting ready for a job interview. We put a lot of notes in our workbooks and last night you made a short list of the important points. I want to review these points today and see if we can make a short listing of the important things we studied. Then we'll put these in our workbooks and on a large poster. The purpose of this short listing is for you to have a guide to study when you leave school and study this workbook."
2. Teacher and students read and discuss notes in workbook, Unit XII, Days 1 and 2. Teacher elicits statements from students to coincide with information presented below.
B. Student activities
1. Students read Unit XII, Days 1 and 2, with teacher and discuss facts fully. Upon completion of short listing on board, students copy material into workbooks.
2. Students make large poster with short listing.
V. Summary
Teacher says, "You can see that there are really five things to remember about going for a job interview. You'll notice that so far we've only talked about getting ready. For the next few days we're going to talk about and study how to act during a job interview."

UNIT XII DAY 3

How to Get Ready for the First Job Interview

(Workbook page 120)
1. Decide where you want to look.
2. Be scared a little—it's all right.

3. Go alone.
4. Be on time.
5. Look your best—like going to church.
   Your boss is looking at you during the interview, trying to decide whether you will be a good worker. Look your best, and act your best.

UNIT XII   DAYS 4, 5 AND 6

Going for Your First Job Interview

   I. Subject: How to act at a job interview
  II. Purpose: To provide a model of alertness for the student to follow.
 III. Materials
     A. Teacher materials
        1. Blackboard and chalk
     B. Student materials
        1. Workbook, Unit XII, Days 4, 5 and 6, pages 121–122
        2. Pencil or pen
 IV. Sequence of lesson
     A. Teacher activities
        1. This material entails three days of presentation. Teacher should continue the presentation for all three days using the same format.
        2. Teacher says, "For the past few days we talked about getting ready for the interview. We now look our Sunday best. We are dressed just right. We are in the boss's office and ready for our interview. The question now is, how do we act? What do we do during the interview? Do we just sit there and act as if we were dead? No, we should act like interesting people. How do you think we should act throughout an interview? Start thinking."
     B. Student activities
        1. Students discuss material and copy each item as completed into their workbooks.

V. Summary

Teacher says, "To make a good impression during the interview is not an easy thing. You must show that you have a good attitude and personality. Try doing this here in school at all times. Learn the habits here. We'll practice the interview by asking you questions so you'll have a chance to get to know them. Tomorrow we'll make a short listing of the way you should act."

UNIT XII   DAYS 4, 5 AND 6

How to Act at an Interview

(Workbook pages 121–122)

Day 4

1. Have nice manners. Answer sir to a man or ma'am to a woman. Act the best you can. Try it in school, over and over.
2. Talk up. Do not just sit there as if you were dead. Answer questions in a strong voice but be relaxed and easy. Offer some thoughts of your own. Show the boss you are thinking.
3. Look awake. Be awake and enthusiastic through the interview. Don't look as if you are sleeping.
4. Tell them why you came to this business. You heard that this is a fair place to work. Some of your friends work here and they spoke very well about this business. You want to work here.

Day 5

5. Tell them that you like this kind of work. That's another reason you came here. You want to do this type of work.
6. Show that you are reliable and dependable. That you almost never were late or absent from school. The company can call your school and see if this is true.
7. Show them that you are willing to work. Let him know that you will work hard and keep trying. Talk about what you learned in these units. This will show that you know how to work hard.

8. Tell them if you have finished high school. This shows that you can finish something you start.

Day 6

9. Tell them why you think you can do the work here. Explain that you like this kind of work.

10. Show them you are responsible, a hard worker who will try to improve and produce more.

11. Show them that you have a good attitude and that you want to succeed and you want a chance to try to prove it.

12. Be enthusiastic. Show them you are a willing person who will be loyal and honest.

UNIT XII   DAY 7

Going for Your First Job Interview

I. Subject: Summary of how to act during a job interview

II. Purpose

   A. To review Days 4, 5 and 6 in Unit XII.

   B. To provide the students with a guideline for "How to Act During a Job Interview."

III. Materials

   A. Teacher materials

      1. Blackboard and chalk

      2. Poster paper and brush pen

   B. Student materials

      1. Workbook, Unit XII, Days 4, 5, 6 and 7

      2. Pencil

IV. Sequence of lesson

   A. Teacher activities

      1. Teacher and students reread Unit XII, Days 4, 5 and 6. Discuss fully all ideas presented.

      2. Teacher says, "For the past three days we have talked about how to act during a job interview. Let's review this information and pull out the main ideas. Then we'll write them on the board and we'll have a short listing of

important ideas to study now and later in life. Then we'll put these in our workbooks and on a poster so a group of you can study them together."
B. Student activities
1. Students discuss Unit XII, Days 4, 5 and 6 with teacher.
2. Students copy material placed on board into workbooks, Unit XII, Day 7, pages 122–123.
3. Students make a poster listing ideas placed on board.
V. Summary
Teacher says, "These twelve ideas are very important for you to remember during a job interview. Most of these same ideas are important to you here in school or on a job. Study them now and after you finish school. For the next few days we're going to talk about the kind of questions you will be asked during a job interview."

UNIT XII DAY 7

How to Act and What to Say at a Job Interview

(Workbook pages 122–123)
1. Use good manners.
2. Talk up clearly.
3. Look awake.
4. Tell why you came here.
5. Show that you like this kind of work.
6. Show that you are reliable and dependable.
7. Show that you are willing.
8. Say that you finished high school (if you did).
9. Show that you can do the work.
10. Show that you are responsible and a hard worker.
11. Show that you have a good attitude, you want to succeed, and you want a chance to prove it.
12. Be enthusiastic.

UNIT XII   DAYS 8 AND 9

Going for Your First Job Interview

   I. Subject: Questions you will be asked during a job interview
  II. Purpose
    A. To provide the student with some idea of the type of question he will have to answer in a job interview.
    B. To provide students with a model of answers to common interview questions.
 III. Materials
    A. Teacher materials
      1. Blackboard and chalk
    B. Student materials
      1. Workbook, Unit XII, Days 8 and 9
      2. Pen or pencil
  IV. Sequence of lesson
    A. Teacher activities
      1. Teacher says, "For the next two days we will talk about some of the kinds of questions you will be asked during an interview. I will put the questions on the board and I want you to give me the answers. Remember to look your best and be awake. The first question will be. . . ." (Prompt for answers and reword as shown below.)
    B. Student activities
      1. Students discuss questions asked by teacher and copy answers into workbooks as each question is completed.
   V. Summary
Teacher says, "These are only some of the questions the boss will ask you. There will be many more questions. You will have to fill out lots of forms. I will tell you more about these. You may have to take a lie-detector test. Always tell the truth and you have nothing to be afraid of. During this questioning your boss will be looking for the things we learned about in these and other units. He wants to decide if you will be a good worker. Show him the best you can do. Tomorrow we will have a story about Ginger, who lost her job."

UNIT XII   DAYS 8 AND 9

Some Questions You Will Be Asked During an Interview

(Workbook pages 123–125)

Day 8

1. What is your name?
1. Give your full name. All of it.

2. Where do you live?
2. Give your full address.

3. How long have you lived here?
3. Tell how many years.

4. How far did you get in school?
4. Tell how long you went to school. If you are completing high school, tell this also.

5. Why did you come here to this business?
5. To look for a job.

6. Why this business?
6. You heard that it is a good place to work. You heard that the things they make here are good. You like to do this kind of work. You picked this business from all the rest to come and look for a job.

Day 9

7. Where have you worked before?
7. Tell him any places you have worked before. Tell him why you left. If you were fired, or quit for poor reasons, it will look bad, but you have to be honest. If this is your first full-time job, tell him you are finishing school and never have worked full-time before.

8. Have you ever had any accidents?
8. Tell the truth. If you have had accidents tell him why. It is better if you have not had any accidents.

9. Can you drive a car?
9. Answer yes only if you have a license.

10. Are you in good health?

10. Answer truthfully. Tell him that you never were late or missed school except for very important reasons. Tell him how many times you were late or absent in school. This can show him that you are reliable and dependable.

11. How much salary do you want?

11. As much as any other beginner. You don't care about salary now. You want the job now so you can show him you can learn to do the job. When you become a good worker and produce more, he can give you a raise. Right now the important thing is to get the job so you will have the chance to show him you can improve and produce.

UNIT XII   DAY 10

Going for Your First Job Interview

   I. Subject: Ginger loses her job
  II. Purpose
      A. To review Unit XII, Day 7.
      B. To present a story embodying and reviewing contents of Unit XII.
 III. Materials
      A. Teacher materials: none
      B. Student materials
         1. Workbook, Unit XII, Days 3, 7 and 10
         2. Notebook and pencil
  IV. Sequence of lesson
      A. Teacher activities
         1. Teacher says, "We are going to do two things today. First, we will go over over Days 3 and 7 in your workbooks. Then we have a story about Ginger."
         2. Review Days 3 and 7 material. Stress important points and make the material very meaningful.
         3. Teacher says, "Here is a story about Ginger. Let's read it and see what happened to her."

B. Student activities

1. Students and teacher read story and discuss important (underlined) ideas.

V. Summary

Teacher says, "Tomorrow we'll have our test on Unit XII. Tonight study the entire unit carefully."

Ginger Loses Her Job

Ginger kept hearing talk that the cleaning plant was moving to another city. Business was bad, and the boss wanted to move to another city where he thought he could make more money. The talk was true. The plant moved and Ginger lost her job. The boss asked her to move to the new city but Ginger did not want to leave her family and Ben. Ginger went looking for a job the day after she lost her job. She went to four cleaning plants before she found a new job. She liked this kind of work and knew how to do it. Here is what Ginger did when she went looking for a job. She took a shower and made sure she was clean. Then she put on a dark dress that she wore to church on Sundays. She wore a little make-up and combed her hair. She looked very nice and neat.

Since Ginger had finished school two years ago, her new boss wanted to know where she had worked, how long, and why she left. He was trying to find out if she was a job jumper, a person who quits many jobs or is fired from them. No employer wants to hire a worker who is a job jumper. When she told him that she had worked at the same cleaning plant for the two years since she had finished high school, he thought that she was reliable. He still wanted to know why she lost her job. He wondered if she had been a good worker for two years and then got lazy. Maybe she had become a troublemaker. When she told him that the plant had moved, and that her old boss had wanted her to move also, he knew that this girl was a dependable worker. He hired her. Ginger was a little scared when she first went to work. It was a new place to her and she did not know the people. She kept quiet, tried hard, and did more than her part of the work. Very soon all the girls she worked with liked her. Her boss was happy with her work. She kept on trying and producing more. Soon he gave her a raise in salary.

Ginger and Ben are still going together. They hope to get married in a year or two. They are both saving their money to buy things they will need when they start their home. They are both working hard and saving as much as they can out of their salaries.

UNIT XII DAY 11

Going for Your First Job Interview

I. Subject: Unit XII test

II. Purpose

A. To review this unit's content through the test method.

B. To test the students' grasp of material presented in this unit.

III. Materials
   A. Teacher materials: none
   B. Student materials
      1. Workbook, Unit XII, Day 11, pages 126–128
      2. Pen or pencil
IV. Sequence of lesson
   A. Teacher activities
      1. Teacher says, "Today we take our test on Unit XII. Let's read the directions together." (After test is completed, collect workbooks.)
   B. Student activities
      1. Students take test on Unit XII, Day 11
 V. Summary
   Teacher says, "I will grade these tests tonight and we will go over them tomorrow."

Test on Unit XII

(Workbook pages 126–128)

Name_____ Date_____

Part 1

If you think the sentence is right, put a line under Yes. If you think the sentence is wrong, put a line under No.

Yes No 1. Look for a job in a business where you will like the work.

Yes No 2. Never be scared of a job interview.

Yes No 3. When you go for a job interview, take a friend with you.

Yes No 4. When you go for a job interview, look neat and clean.

Yes No 5. When you go for a job interview, wear dirty old clothes.

Yes No 6. During the interview act dumb.

Yes No 7. During the interview try to show that you are reliable.

Yes No 8. Look and act awake during the interview—not asleep.

Yes No 9. Try to tell the boss some of the things you learned in these units.

Yes No 10. Ask for a chance to show you can do the work and produce more.

Part 2

Tell what you can do to get ready before you go for a job interview.
1. Decide where you want to look.
2. Don't worry about being a little scared.
3. Go alone.
4. Be on time.
5. Look your best.

Part 3

How should you act while the interview is going on?
1. Use good manners.
2. Talk clearly.
3. Look awake.
4. Tell why you came here.
5. Tell why you like this kind of work.
6. Show you are reliable and dependable.
7. Show that you are willing.
8. Tell that you finished high school, if you did.
9. Show that you can do the work.
10. Show that you are responsible and a hard worker.
11. Show that you have a good attitude and want to succeed and a chance to prove it.
12. Be enthusiastic.

Part 4

How would you answer these questions during an interview?
1. Where did you last work?
   Tell the truth.
2. Why did you leave there?
   Tell the truth.

3. Why did you come to this business for a job?
   I am interested in this kind of work.
4. How much salary do you want?
   As much as any new worker.
5. Can you show me if you are reliable and dependable?
   My records in school can prove this.
6. Why do you think you can do this work?
   I am interested in this kind of work and I think I can do it.
7. How much schooling have you had?
   I finished high school and my last teacher was ——————.
8. How can I know if you are a safe worker?
   I never had any trouble or accidents in school or on my last job.
9. How do I know if you are telling the truth?
   Call my teacher or last employer.
10. Why should I hire you and not someone else?
    I am interested in this work and am reliable and will be loyal
    to this business.

UNIT XII   DAY 12

Going for Your First Job Interview

I. Subject: Review of test on Unit XII
II. Purpose
   A. To review contents of Unit XII.
   B. To provide students a correct set of answers to serve as a
      guide in adult life.
III. Materials
   A. Teacher materials
      1. Blackboard and chalk
   B. Student materials
      1. Workbook, Unit XII, Day 11
      2. Pen or pencil
IV. Sequence of lesson
   A. Teacher activities
      1. Teacher returns workbooks to students and discusses test

with students, providing correct answers. Discuss fully questions on which students had greatest difficulty.

B. Student activities
   1. Students discuss test with teacher and correct incorrect answers in workbooks.

V. Summary

Teacher says, "We have now finished these units. Take these workbooks home and read them often. The ideas in these workbooks are very important to you in your adult lives. They will help you to keep your jobs and be successful. Never lose these books. Read them whenever you go for a job or whenever you begin to think, How can I get ahead or How can I do better in my job and be a happier person?"